THE CHANGING SCENE

THE CHANGING SCENE

MEMOIRS OF A CIVIL SERVANT

CHANDRA BHUSHAN PRASAD
IAS (Retd.)

Commonwealth

The Changing Scene

ISBN : 81-7169-221-4

Edition : 2020

Published by **:**
COMMONWEALTH PUBLISHERS (P) LTD.
4831/24, Govind Lane,
Ansari Road, Darya Ganj,
New Delhi - 110002
Ph. : 23272541, 23242541
e-mail : commonwealthpublishers2016@gmail.com

Distributed by :
ARJUN PUBLISHING HOUSE
4831/24, Govind Lane,
Ansari Road, Darya Ganj,
New Delhi - 110002
Ph. : 23272541, 23242541
e-mail : arjunbooks2001@gmail.com

Laser Typesetting by :
Dimple Computers
Delhi

Printed at :
Divine Digital Press
Delhi

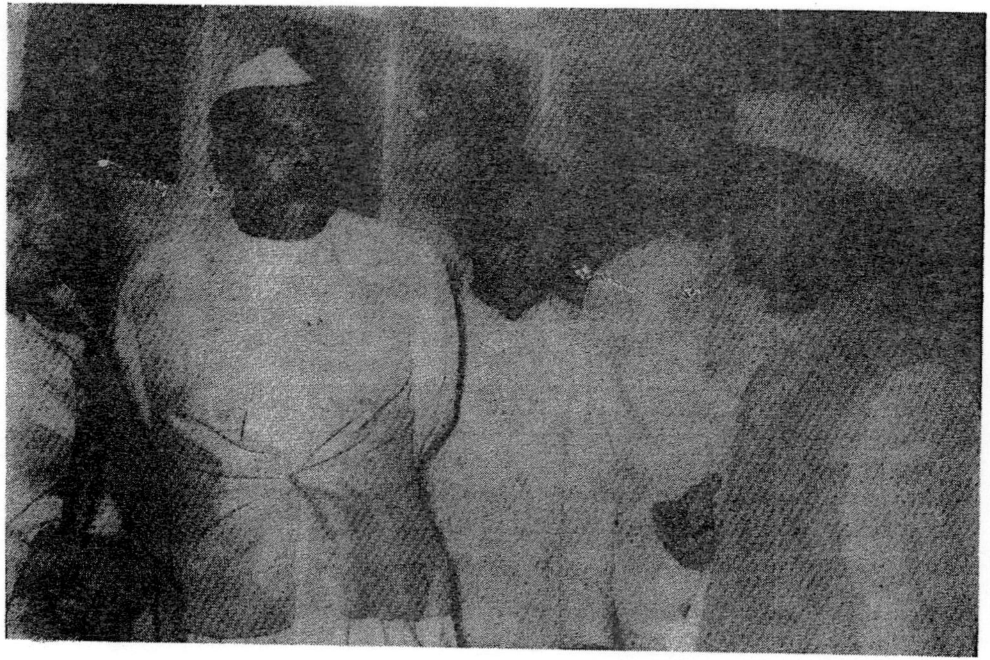

The Prime Minister Lal Bahadur Shastri talking to the author on the occasion of the inauguration of the Bihar Information Centre at New Delhi on 27-4-65
The Chief Minister, Shri K.B. Sahay is also seen in the Picture

The author inaugurating the Seminar on Export Potentialities of Minor Minerals at Goa in Singhbhum District on 21-12-74

The author with Pressmen in his Office at Patna

The author's wife (Srimati Bindhya vasini Prasad) whose memory the book has been dedicated

IN
the loving memory of my wife
BINDI
(Late Bindhyavasini Prasad)

Preface

1st January, 1979 I have laid down my office this morning having reached the age of 58 years on the 22nd December, 1978, but continued till the end of the month under the new superannuation rules under which a Government servant lays down his office on the last day of the month in which his retirement falls due. These nine days, the days of grace, have been quite uneventful like most days during the last one year of my service, except that I have been somewhat busy filling up countless number of forms and statements to enable me to get the various retirement benefits in time.

I had never thought that I would write my reminiscences much less have them published. But I have been so shaken during the last few years of my service by the fall in the general standards that I have hesitatingly decided, under great pressure from my wife and some of my close friends to write down some of my experiences which would throw some light on the falling health of the administration in Bihar during the last four decades. The intention, however, is not to find fault with individuals, be they Civil Servants or Politicians ; but to portray the events as they took place, which bring out the functioning of the administrative apparatus and the individuals controlling it at various levels in sharp focus. I would, however, sound a note of caution and also offer my apologies in advance as the whole narrative is based mainly on memory ; and so the possibility of slight deviation here and there cannot be ruled out. But the incidents and situations detailed in the narrative are basically and broadly correct. There is yet another indulgence which I would crave of my readers. This narrative is a personal memoir, and so the obnoxious first person singular is bound to occur countless number of times. This will naturally be exasperating ; but the odium of going through an autobiographical sketch will have to be borne.

I hope that this narrative of an ordinary civil servant will excite some thinking among the Junior members of the Civil Services and the right thinking public men, who will make a concerted effort to salvage the administrative apparatus in Bihar, as elsewhere including the Central Government, because I implicitly believe that the administrators of this State who brought the distinction of Bihar being one of the best governed states in the country, can do it again and achieve greater distinction than before.

I also owe it to my readers to explain why this narrative is being published years after my retirement from service. The work was completed quite some time ago, but a sense of modesty and awe prevented me from rushing into a realm 'where angels fear to tread', for I have neither been a Civil Servant of much distinction nor a writer at all to boast of. But my friends and well wishers continued to prod me to have it published. And it is not unnatural for a man in his seventies to succumb to such pressures when a sneaking desire to be known outside his own immediate circle also seems to overtake him. So the book is now before you for whatever it might be worth.

Before concluding, I would like to place on record my deep sense of gratitude to my friend Shri Shivanugrah Narain, a retired judge of Patna High Court, who kindly went through the draft and encouraged me to have this memoir published. I must also express my appreciation to Shri Surendra Bahadur, a retired Joint Director of the Public Relations Department and a friend of mine for the meticulous care with which he went through the typed copy of the manuscript. My son, Ashok Kumar and my son-in-law R.K. Sinha, both of the Indian Administrative Service, also deserve mention for helping me in this endeavour.

Date : 18th July 1992

Chandra Bhushan Prasad

Contents

1

Recruitment and Training

I do not know how far it is correct to make recruitment to the Indian Administrative Service through various sources. There are the regular recruits, the various types of emergency recruits, the special recruits and the promotees from the State Civil Service and other Services. This has, among other things, led to a lack of cohesion in the service and has often presented a picture of a house divided in different compartments. The regular recruits consider themselves superior to all, and often look down upon even special recruits as interlopers and inferior to them in merit. The special recruits i.e. those who entered the service through the Special Recruitment Examination, 1956—all of age group senior to the regular recruits—being small in number often find themselves isolated and are looked askance both by the regular recruits as well as by the promotees. The promotees consider themselves as a class apart and their general outlook and performances often betray complexes of their past service. They are popular with elected governments, as it is felt that they are more pliable than others and can safely be relied upon by politicians. Though from this class have also come out some of the most illustrious members of the service, the rank and file amongst them have been content to remain 'howers of wood and drawers of water'—ready to take the command and execute it with greater zeal and vehemence than what even the authors of the Scheme had contemplated.

I was recruited to the IAS through the Special recruitment examination, 1956 and joined the IAS staff college, Simla in

July, 1958. We were in all 62 trainees, all coming from different walks of life, from all over the country including half a dozen nominees from the state of Jammu and Kashmir. In this batch of 62, there were about forty pages with foreign training, degree or diploma from a foreign University and nearly half the number had a doctorate in some subject or the other. They came from Government Service, from business firms, from the universities and the farms. The vice principal, Dr. G. Jacob, IAS (a Bihar civilian), who was to all intents and purposes the principal of the college, as there was no principal, a man of profound learning and vast experience, often used to exclaim that never in his life had he met such a distinguished lot of people—all at a time under him. Quite a few others who came from Delhi to lecture to the class often spoke in the same vein.

The period of training at the staff college (a condensed course for the special recruits) from July, 1958 to Jan., 1959 was one of the happiest and most fruitful periods of my service life. Dr Jacob and other professors and teachers treated us more as colleagues and we felt absolutely at ease with them. The after-lecture hours were often spent playing cards with Dr. Jacob and Dr. Rao, a young teacher of Sociology Mr. Pathak who taught us law had such a fine knack of teaching law that we learnt and remembered most of it while he was lecturing in the class room. The other teachers were also good and helpful. I still recollect the paternal advice given to us by Dr. Jacob when he met us in small groups at a farewell tea at his residence on completion of our course in the college. The encouragement given by Dr. Jacob gave me the confidence to face the new challenge in my role as an administrator on my posting in Bihar.

Life in the staff college was full of fun and activities from morning till evening. Apart from the regular classes, we had lectures by eminent administrators from Delhi and other places, Seminars and Syndicate studies, and the usual 'dinners' teas and 'service nights', etc. We had one or two excursions also mainly around Himachal Pradesh and Punjab. Life was full, youthful and fanciful all through, though I had to put in some hard labour at the end of the term for the passing out examination at the close of the training. Incidentally, I secured very high marks alongwith some others in most subjects, like Law, Economics, Sociology etc., and got Al ranking for my overall performance though I never considered myself as one among the distinguished few. When the allotment order came from the Ministry of Home Affairs, my year of allotment was 1953 and I was posted to my Home State, Bihar. Six more including Nandeshwar Prasad, another Bihari, who also superannuated on the same day as I, were allotted to the Bihar Cadre.

On completion of our academic course in the IAS Staff College Simla, we were brought to Delhi and put up in the Administrative Training School meant for the annual regular recruits for our meeting with the President, Prime Minister, Home Minister and our attachment with some of the Ministries of the Government of India. Dr. Rajendra Prasad was then the President of India. The Secretary to the President who wrote to Dr. Jacob fixing the appointment added a postcript saying that the President would be happy if the officers appeared in Khadi. Since I had not thought of this and had no Khadi outfit, I hurriedly purchased a ready made woollen Khadi coat from the Khadi Emporium in Delhi.

The meeting with the President was a homely affair. The atmosphere of informality even in the Rashtrapati Bhavan spoke volumes about the incumbent—his simple unostentatious living and childlike sincerity and candour. After the formal address by the President which lasted but a few minutes, Rajendra Babu asked us to have a look around the Rashtrapati Bhavan and the Moghal Garden.

The next meeting, that with Prime Minister, Jawaharlal Nehru was really an exciting affairs. We made vast mental preparations because we did not know what Pandit Nehru would ask and from whom, and what predicament the man would be in if the PM asked some inconvenient questions. But the meeting passed off extremely well. Pandit Nehru who had given the time at 7 PM came in the room just on the dot at seven, and after having exchanged a few pleasantries with Dr. Jacob and with us, plunged into a most beautiful and exhilarating speech which lasted well over half an hour. The exhortation which he gave us still keeps ringing in my ears, His ideas of what he expected from the administrators will provide a beacon light to the future generations of civil servants.

During our meeting with Pandit Nehru a very funny, (though of some concern) incident happened. One of our colleagues, TB Singh, an officer from Darjeeling side, started vomitting right at the residence of the PM. We were a little upset but the PM, when he came to know of it, coolly advised his personal attendant to take TB Singh to the bathroom and to make him at ease.

Our next meeting—with the Home Minister, Pandit Gobind Ballabh Pant was a great flop. The Home Minister appeared in our midst nearly two hours later than the time fixed by him though he was sitting in another room of the same house (his official residence) while we were waiting in the drawing room. Nothing of substance was talked at the meeting with the Home Minister, though the recruitments, training and posting etc., of the All India Services is a matter falling within the sphere of work of the Ministry of Home Affairs.

Of the round of meetings we had with the senior officials of the Government of India, the one we had with Sri Vishnu Sahay, Cabinet Secretary and Secretary of the Planning Commission was the most rewarding. I, along with a few of my colleagues, was attached with the Planning Commission for a week or so. Shri Sahay was not only a stalwart by physical standards but also struck me to be an intellectual gaint, a man bubbling with energy all the time. He also struck me as an understanding and straight forward type and gave as, in his usual small talks, some real inklings into the working of the Planning Commission and the Government of India as a whole.

Early in February, 1959, we the Bihar officers, reported to the Department of Personnel, then called the Appointment Department. I was full of excitement, as I was coming to my home state to serve now in a new capacity to posts involving various types of challenges, and looked forward to meaningful cooperation and assistance from my colleagues and superiors.

Shri M S Rao ICS, the then Chief Secretary received us with enthusiasm and kindness and so did some others like the late Shri T.P. Singh, ICS who became the Chief Secretary later. But my experiences with some Junior Officers of the IAS was chilling. In my very first meeting with an Under Secretary in the Appointment Department, who incidentally ranked much Junior to me, a direct recruit who had already done a sub-division and was now in the Appointment Department, often jibed at us saying that while he had earned his seniority by being in the service, we the special recruits had our seniority thrust upon us. Another thing that attracted my notice soon after my posting in Bihar was that leaving aside the promoted officers whose cases obviously are a little different, there was a general feeling that the State Government showed a marked preference to the non-Bihari IAS Officers, in matters of postings and transfers to key posts, who generally got the cream of postings. One of the reasons obviously was that the Ministers generally preferred non-Bihari officers if Bihari officers of their own castes were not available. I say this with anguish as the malady which had just made its appearance when I entered IAS started gripping the administrative apparatus and became so pronounced as the years rolled by that even a casual visitor to the state could spot this out in no time. This Cancer of casteism in administration the beginning of which was made even during the last days of Late Shri Krishna Sinha, went on developing with great strides, no matter which party ruled Bihar, until at last it took a malignant form and burst out in the open during the time of Shri Karpoori Thakur in the closing years of the seventies, when the cult of 'backward' and 'forward' divided the services into two distinct blocks, as a sequel to the much flaunted principle of making reservations in the services for the so called backward classes on the analogy of reservation for the Scheduled Castes and scheduled tribes. It is hardly within the scope of this narrative to dwell upon in detail the relative merits of the arguments of the protagonists of the policy of reservation and those opposed to it. The spokesman of the upper castes wanted this special treatment to all economically weaker sections of the society irrespective of the castes to which they belonged, while the leaders of the backward castes vociferously pleaded for confining the benefits to the members of the backward castes alone. Every student of Sociology knows that the caste structure and the economic structure are such that they often Coalesce at a certain point; and whether you make reservations on the basis of caste or economic backwardness the net result will in effect be more or less the same—the backward castes getting the bulk of the reserved vacancies. But politicians are generally averse to finding a real solution to such vexed questions. A very ominous trend in the whole affair was that the real implication of the reservation policy was never explained to the people and the matter was allowed to drift. The so called forward castes were, therefore, led to believe that apart from the vacancies reserved for the backward castes, the candidates of backward castes would encroach upon the unreserved vacancies too if some of them were high up in the merit list. This was not the accepted formula for filling up the reserved vacancies even in respect of the Scheduled castes and the tribes. During the period when the agitation by the forward castes was at the highest pitch and when strikes, processions and bandhs were the order of the day, I suggested to a state Minister belonging to a high caste to get a press note issued explaining how the policy would in effect, work. The Minister was surprised that he did not know of this that if a member of the backward caste competed in order of merit there would be one less seat reserved for the backward castes. He spoke to the Chief Minister on my suggestion and later confided in me that the Chief Minister had asked him not to make this point public as it would annoy the leaders of the backward castes. This is an instance how the Government in Bihar ran during the closing years of the seventies. This is, however, a digression and I find that I have jumped to the closing years of my service without first dwelling on the events preceding them.

On completion of the course of training in the Staff College and after having an initial round of meetings for getting to know the things in the secretariat I was posted as an Assistant Magistrate and Collector (later redesignated as

Joint Magistrate and Collector in view of my seniority) at Gaya. A.F. Couto, the then District Magistrate was an old acquaintance having been SDO of Jamshedpur when I was posted there as an Assistant Commissioner of Labour prior to my entry into the IAS.

Couto was a fine man, an understanding boss, and a pleasant colleague. He made me feel quite at home in my new environment and treated me with such consideration that I often felt and so did others, as if I was the second collector of the district. Due to my seniority (the year of allotment being 1953 during which year Couto also entered the IAS), I habitually received more than the usual respect due to an IAS trainee. The training was more in the nature of going through the various aspects of administration as a matter of routine. But I got the hang of most Departments in the collectorate because Couto often associated me in decision making and even ordered the officers to take instructions from me, if he himself happened to be away. An important assignment that he gave me during this period was to place me in overall charge of the arrangements in connection with the visit of the President of India, Dr. Rajendra Prasad, to the Sheokhodeora Ashram of Shri Jai Prakash Narayan in Nawadah Sub-Division in early 1959. Mr. S.V. Sohoni, ICS who later became the Chief Secretary, and after his retirement, the Lokayukta of Bihar, was then the Commissioner of Patna Division. Mr. Sohoni also knew me from before and we were almost family friends for many many years to come. We were all camping at Shekhodeora and seeing to the minutest details of the arrangements. On the day the President was to arrive in the afternoon, J.P. had been out supervising the arrangements as the President was to be his quest during his stay at Shekhodeora. Seeing us at the local Dak Bungalow nearby, he came to meet Mr. Sohoni, and when he started going back to the ashram Mr. Sohoni asked me to drive JP in our jeep to his residence. While I was driving JP to his Ashram, the jeep skidded badly at a turning and very nearly over-turned; but fortunately nothing untoward happened and JP got out of the jeep smiling; and we again resumed our journey to the

Ashram where we reached safely. I was quite shaken thinking that if anything serious had happened I would have got a stigma and would have felt guilty all my life. On my return to the Dak Bungalow, I mentioned this to Mr. Sohoni who thanked God for averting this unfortunate situation. However, he jocularly advised me never to attempt to drive any V.I.P. even if asked to do so, an advice I have scrupulously followed except during my short posting at Purnea, when the then Chief Minister, Pandit Binodanand Jha, always insisted on my driving the car and sitting beside me in the front seat. Curiously enough, JP never mentioned this to anybody, and when I told about this to Prabhawati ji, JP's wife, next day, she expressed absolute surprise and ignorance about the matter as JP had not mentioned any thing about it even to her.

During the period of my training at Gaya, N.K. Bhardwaj the SDO of Aurangabad went on a month's leave for his marriage. Couto had me officiate as the SDO of Aurangabad during Bhardwaj's absence.

2

Sub-Divisional Offices—the First Tests of General Administration

Soon after my term as SDO Aurangabad concluded, I was posted in July 1959 as subdivisional officer of Araria in the District of Purnea. Araria had the reputation of being a very troublesome subdiuision, and with constant friction between the land owners and the sikmidars, the Hindus and the Muslims, and the clandestine trade with Nepal through Forbesganj and Jogbani on the Indo-Nepal border, it had become a problem subdivision and had put several sub-divisional officers in trouble. Being a sub-division bordering Nepal, it had during the British rule generally been an ICS station and had the distinction of having had as its SDO, some of the distinguished members of the Service, like Shri Bhagwan Sahay who subsequently became our Ambassador in Nepal, Shri Gokhale and many important Britishers. The subdivision had some very big land owning families, and officers who succumbed to the lure of good food, lavish hospitality and fast life which life in far-flung and remote areas could easily provide, often got into trouble. Shri B. Narayana, IAS was dismissed from the service on charges which related to the period of his posting in Araria. Two other officers who succeeded him and whose names must remain anonymous as one of them still is in service also got into serious trouble. However, during the entire period of my posting at Araria for nearly one and a half years I felt extremely happy and I still remember with great satisfaction the manifold work of relief succour to the poor, of nipping the mischief of the trouble makers in the bud, and of my exhilirating tours in the remote interior. When I recall the events and experiences of various positions and places during my entire career, the period spent at Araria stands out prominently as one of the most pleasant and satisfying periods of my life.

Araria then, and to a large extent even now, is a backward place. The subdivisional headquarters had no electricity and no running water supply and very little else by way of amenities which go with modern life. There was an apology of a market, the nearest tolerable market being Forbesganj, 20 miles away, a small hospital, a high school housed in a rickety building, and a few government quarters emitting light from petromax lamps and lanterns in the evening. The SDO's residence, an old style thatched roofed building of well over fifty years, though small was comfortable, surrounded by a Mango orchard having well over three dozen mango trees, was the meeting place of the officials at the end of the days work. The local contingent of officers comprised, besides the SDO, of a second officer, the subdivisional police officer, called the Deputy Superintendent of Police, an Inspector of Police a SDO of PWD, the Hospital Doctor, two Munsifs, the local BDO, and of course the Thana Contingent. Most of these often met for tea or dinner at the residence of one of the officers. This was all the social life.

We had few good roads in the subdivision. The road connecting Araria with Purnea and continuing upto Forbesganj and Jogbani in the opposite direction was the only metalled road in the subdivision, besides the one connecting Forbesganj with Narpatganj block. During both the years (1959 and 1960) that I was posted there, I had to tour the villages during the rains on bullock carts, 'bhainsa carts', boats, horse back and elephants, apart from a good deal of hitch hiking. But there was a great compensating factor in the midst of this arduous life. Except in Araria proper and Forbesganj, where there were nests of unscrupulous and troublesome persons, the people by and large were extremely good, and the more I toured in the countryside the more I felt convinced that the average villager had a respect for integrity and good work. I am by nature reserved in my private life and I made it a principle not to accept private hospitality. During the entire period of my posting as SDO Araria and subsequently as Collector of Purnea, I cannot recall a single instance at which I was a guest of honour at a private party or joined the same during the visit of some VIP. This practice I kept up more or less during the rest of my life while in Government service. I think that too much mixing with the well-to-do sections of the society is not only unethical but also administratively unsound because it does create a doubt among the poor and the less affluent whether they can really expect uninhibited justice when the interest of the rich and the poor, the landlords and the tenants, the big land owners and their sikmidars clashed. I firmly believe that senior officers must not only be honest but should also by their conduct make people believe that they are honest. And who can seriously claim that those who habitually accept parties from the rich and the affluent, dine in private houses and stay in the homes of the well-to-do and influential persons can really maintain their impartiality when the cases of these people are involved? I actually came across instances of definite abuse of power on the part of a very senior officer in favour of a rich land owner with whom he was on friendly terms, and from whom he and members of his family accepted lavish hospitality. Of this, however, I shall speak later.

Since Araria provided the formative years of my career in the IAS, I feel tempted to recall a few instances of handling of certain situations as they cropped up, and their reaction among the public at large.

Because of the multiplicity of problems and paucity of officers, life in the subdivision was quite arduous. Case work was quite heavy as there had been no separation of the judicial function, and floods, fire and agrarian disputes took a lot of our time. The Second officer, Shri S.N. Verma was of considerable assistance and provided me with the much needed relief in case work. Shri S.N. Haider (now deceased) was, though not so popular with the officers and the general public for his forthright and sometimes overbearing manners, did his best to relieve me of some of my worries, in revenue administration. The official life, however, was greatly smoothened by the very kind and humane attitude of my District Magistrate, Shri S.K. Chakravarti whom I regard as one of the most considerate officers I have had chance to work with. He had always a kind word of appreciation for all those who did their work consientiously. His successor, Shri R.N. Mitra was a Constitutional collector—timid and non-interfering and was chary of taking decisions in difficult matters. On the whole he was a good man and our relations were very cordial.

Yes, I was going to recount a few of the incidents which still appear fresh in my memory.

Araria subdivision has a substantial muslim population, and Forbesganj town was notorious for recurring incidents of communal tension often generated by throwing of beef in some public places like the compound of some temple, street hydrants, etc. This was a source of constant headache and very often I had to wake up at unearthly hours, between midnight and dawn, to attend to such situations. All of us were so fed up with this nuisance that I decided to call it a day by taking some abrupt action. One evening, I called the sub-Inspecter of Police In charge of Forbesganj Police Station and asked him to give a proposal for banning cow slaughter for a limited period in and around Forbesganj; and I signed an order under section 144 Cr. PC prohibiting the killing of cows and calves, bullocks etc. within a radius of five miles of Forbesganj town for 5 days. I also had the order announced by beat of drum in and around Forbesganj the same night and the order came into force immediately. This order came unexpectedly and there was a great hue and cry from the Muslims. A large number of telegrams, letters and representations were sent to the Collector, the chief Minister and even the Prime Minister of India. The Muslims argued that this order infringed on their religious rights. A revision against my order was also filed in the court of the District Magistrate of Purnea. But slaughter of cows etc., stopped immediately and before the District Magistrate had time to hear the revision petition, the force of the order expired, and the revision petition became infructuous. On the expiry of this order, however, I passed a fresh order which remained in force for another week. Whatever might be the merit or otherwise of this drastic step taken by me, the effect was salutary and instances of throwing of beef, etc. stopped and did not recur till I remained at Araria.

The next interesting incident was provided during the annual Moharram festival in 1960. During the previous few years, a convention had grown that to enable the Tazias of abnormal heights to pass unhindered, electric and telegraph wires were lowered throughout Forbesganj town on the 10th day of Moharram on which processions were taken out. In 1960, as usual, the Muslims demanded that Electric wires and the telegraph wires should be lowered on the Moharram day to enable Tazias to pass through the town unhindered. Since the District Administration had in the past erred in acceding to such a request, the Muslims claimed it on the ground of precedence. In my opinion, this was an unreasonable demand which had no religious force behind it. I considered this question in its various ramifications, and came to the conclusion that while telegraph wires could be lowered tamporarily, we could not agree to the lowering of the electric wires due to several complications which might result in, possible claims by cold storages and others for damages due to wilful disconnection of electricity resulting in loss to them. I, therefore, informed the Tazia Committee of my considered views in the matter. I advised them to reduce the size of their Tazias, if any, to enable them to pass under the electric lines, or alternatively to choose a different route for the procession where the electric wires did not have to be lowered. There was one such route available and the reasonable lot among the Muslims seemed to consider this proposal. But the zealots among them were in no mood to listen to this suggestion and adopted an uncompromising attitude. There was a great hue and cry against my decision and the District Magistrate, R.N. Mitra, who seemed to be in a yielding mood started a dialogue with them. I wrote a letter to the District Magistrate in which I pointed out the danger of agreeing to such an unreasonable demand. The District Magistrate who, by nature, was chary of taking any responsibility in any crucial matter, forwarded my letter to the Government for their orders. Fortunately, the Government (Shri Krishna Sinha was the Chief Minister then) approved of my views with a rider that I should take the responsibility for any untoward incident, should it arise as a result of this decision. I was quite convinced of my stand and set myself to the task of making foolproof arrangements regarding maintenance of law and order during the crucial days that were to follow. The tenth day of Moharram, the day on which the procession with the Tazias was to be taken out at Forbesganj and the areas around were full of excitement with all types of wild rumours gripping the people and even the officials felt diffident. However, we made a careful deployment of the armed forces at our disposal and requisitioned several sections from the District Headquarters and deployed them along with the Lathi Police uuder Magistrates at various strategic points. The road leading to the two—the main route of the procession, was lined with Lathi Constables with sections of armed Police at every point of intersection. I also requested the SP and the DM to start despatching a few sections of armed forces from Purnea to reach Forbesganj from the time the procession was due to enter the town in open jeeps so that the trouble shooters might be given to believe that more and more force was pouring in, so as to deter them from taking recourse to any adventurous action. The Dy. Superintendent of Police, a frail old gentleman, who was feeling extremely nervous was made to camp in the Forbesganj Dak Bungalow and I went round along with my driver supervising the arrangements so that the Muslims were not handicapped in any way in taking out the Tazias. A few troublemakers amongst the Taziya wallas tried to create some commotion but sensing the firm attitude of the authorities the rank and file decided to follow the sensible course. While the procession was about to enter the town, I met the processionist alone and walked a few steps with them joining them in the celebration. The crowd, several thousand strong surged forwad, shook hands with me and gave me a tremendous ovation. After the procession passed off peacefully and a great celebration took place at the Karbala maidan, a few leaders of the Muslims came to see me and congratulated me for the excellent arrangements made for maintenance of law and order during the festival. On receipt of the Khairiat report (all well) the Government, the Commissioner and the District Magistrate all felt relieved and were pleased with my handling of the situation. The District Magistrate came down to Araria on the following day to congratulate me personally and convey the appreciation of the Commissioner. This incidentally set the pattern for handling of such processions in future.

Another incident though of a different nature, which stands out clearly before my mind was regarding an Agrarian dispute. In Forbesganj P.S, in Ramai Village, Shri Mathuranand Thakur was a big cultivator owning hundreds of acres of land. Towards the end of 1959, or early in 1960, at the time of harvesting of paddy crops there was same dispute between him and the Bataidars. Mathuranand Thakur threatened the Bataidars by dangling his own gun before them and even fired a few rounds in the air to scare them away. The Bataidars became panicky and one of them ran to Forbesganj and phoned me up from there. I asked him to report the matter to the Police Station. I despatched the second officer to the site of the occurrence and called for a report from the Thana at once on which I passed an order that Shri Mathuranand Thakur should deposit his gun for safe custody in the Treasury Malkhana within 24 hours, failing which his gun would be seized. I instructed the second officer to camp there with the armed force, promulgate an order under Sec.144 Cr. PC, get the paddy harvested and entrust the same to the Mukhia for division of the produce between the land owner and the Bataidars in accordance with the Law. There was an appeal against my order for seizure of the gun though on receipt of the order, Shri Mathuranand Thakur himself came and deposited the gun in the Treasury. But nothing untoward happened. The paddy was harvested and divided between the contending parties. After this was done, I released the gun of Shri Mathuranand Thakur. This incident had a salutary effect in the villages and we did not hear of such harassment of subtenants during that season. Later on, when I visited the village where the Deputy Minister of Education, Shri Krishna Kant Singh went to inaugurate a school started by Shri Mathuranand Thakur, Shri Thakur was all attention to me and did not even mention about this incident to the Minister who I was told was one of his close relations. At the time of my transfer from Araria at the end of December 1960, there was a tremendous show of respect and affection for me at the time of my making over charge of my office. Thousands of people collected in the Court Compound most of them jostling with one another to try to touch my feet. This token of appreciation of the work done by me for the poor and the down trodden shall ever remain in my memory. In this crowd was also present Shri Mathuranand Thakur of whom I have mentioned earlier. I noticed him rushing forward in the crowd and trying to touch my feet alongwith hundreds of them. I felt overwhelmed and be-wildered at his conduct because apparently I had done him no special favour. As a matter of fact as mentioned in the preceding paragraph I had ordered for seizure of his gun and had his paddy harvested and the produce divided between him and the Bataidars. This action the seizure of his gun, according to a mistaken sense of values prevalent in the countryside was considered a social stigma and lowered the person concerned in the estimation of his fellow men. On my asking Mathuranand Thakur openly told me that by ordering for the seizure of his gun I had saved him from a possible crime and for the fair decision regarding the division of the produce, he felt an unbounded gratitude to me.

My story of Araria will not be complete without mentioning a few things about my District Magistrates Shri S.K. Chakravarti, and his successor, Shri R.N. Mitra and the Divisional Commissioners of Bhagalpur Division, first Dr. Jacob, and then his successor Shri Rameshwar Prasad.

Certain matters regarding Shri S.K. Chakravarti, though seemingly amusing bring forth an aspect of his approach to administration which throw light on his personality in all its dimensions. Shri Chakravarti had the habit of touring all the three sub-divisions, Araria, Kishanganj and Katihar, all within thirty miles from Purnea in different directions almost every day. Araria almost always was his last port of call and was sometimes fortunate to have him spending the night there. His visits though apparently of a routine nature were always valuable because the few minutes he generally spent with me as well as with other SDOs were spent in reviewing the law and order position in the subdivision and the measures to be taken to relieve distress and render succour to the poor and the needy during flood, fire and other natural calamities. It was often a curious sight seeing half a dozen indigent persons coming out of the back of the Land Rover of the D.M., a phenomenon which startled me in the beginning. Very often the persons concerned were victims of fire and needed to be given immediate relief or a landless person in need of some administrative help. Such was the solicitude of Shri Chakravarti for the poor and the needy.

My relations with both Mr. Chakravarti and Mr. R.N.Mitra were excellent. Mr. Chakravarti was a bachelor, but we were on visiting terms with our families during the time of R.N. Mitra.

Both the Commissioners Dr. Jacob and Shri Rameshwar Prasad were specifically kind to me and treated me with great consideration. Dr. Jacob, who knew my wife also while I was under training at the IAS staff college Simla during which period my wife was along with me for quite some time, used to go straight inside the house to meet my wife whom he treated as a daughter. Shri Rameshwar Prasad who succeeded him had also a high opinion of me and came to visit me at my house; and since I did not see any picture in any Cinema House of Araria, he always took me to Katihar to witness a film with him. I had excellent relations with both of them.

3

Industries and Technical Education Problems and Perspectives

After serving my tenure as SDO, I was transferred as an Addl. Director of Industries, Bihar, Patna in the senior scale of the IAS. My tenure of posting as Addl. Director of Industries, during which period I also officiated as the Director of Industries for a month during the incumbent's absence on leave was full of many unsavoury experiences and was an eye opener to me how senior officers who were widely known as 'A' class officers for their efficiency and good work were willy-nilly parties to transactions causing sometimes gains to private persons at the cost of the public exchequer. One of the subjects under my charge was Technical Education including Engineering colleges, Engineering schools, Industrial training, Institutes etc. Of the other two sections, sericulture and power looms also under my charge, the former was clean enough, but the latter under the Taxtile Expert had been involved in some shabby deals in the past one of which caught my attention. It led ultimately to the initiation of departmental proceedings against the Textile Expert, which dragged on for years. I understand that he was one of the officers who was compulsorily retired from service. He was, however, reinstated when the Janata Government came to power and got a review of all cases of compulsory retirement made by a retired High Court judge.

All did not seem to be well with the Section of the Technical Education Wing dealing with Engineering Schools and Colleges. Some of the officers and senior staff at the headquarters as well as some of the Principals of Engineering Colleges and Schools with which this section was concerned had many uncomplementary things to say about the working of this section, particularly in respect of purchase of equipments for the Engineering Schools and Colleges, which to all intents and purposes was a close preserve of the Dy. Director and his Assistant Director. But nobody dared question their bonafide openly as the Dy. Director enjoyed the confidence of the Industries Secretary, Shri B.N. Sinha, IAS, who was widely believed to be one of the ablest officers under the Bihar Government and was quite close to Dr. Sri Krishna Sinha, the then Chief Minister. Shri R.S. Mandal, the then Director of Industries who later became the Chief Secretary and Shri Nageshwar Prasad Singh who succeeded him dealt with the matter of purchases in a rather routine manner. The other Section dealing with Industrial Training Institutes functioned admirably well under a separate Dy. Director who managed his charge with great credit.

After the death of Dr. Shrikrishna Sinha, Pt. Binodanand Jha became the Chief Minister of Bihar and kept the portfolio of Industries under himself and appointed Shri Kamaldeo Narayan Sinha, a legislator from Purnea District, as the Deputy Minister in place of Shri Laliteshwar Prasad Sahi who was the Deputy Minister of Industries when I joined the Department. I found Shri Laliteshwar Prasad Sahi a good man and an intelligent Minister at that.

Soon thereafter, the question of making payments to the suppliers of equipments for the Engineering Schools and Colleges engaged my attention. Some of the Principals of Engineering Schools and Colleges complained to me that several of the equipments supplied did not conform to the specifications laid down in the tender notices and were undoubtedly of sub-standard quality, but they were still being pressurised to accept them and make payments for the same. And they sought my instructions in the matter. In the meantime, the file regarding payment for the purchases came to me with the suggestion that payment for the supplies made should be approved as work in the institutions was suffering in the absence of these equipments, and the financial year was also drawing to a close. I did not feel happy about the whole affair and asked the Principals to withhold payment for the equipments which did not conform to the specifications laid down, till Government orders in the matter were obtained. I could not see my way to agree with the proposals regarding payment, and submitted the file for obtaining the orders of the Chief Minister who also held the portfolio of Industries and Technical Education.

The Director of Industries and the Secretary, Industries who did not want to be involved in the matter passed on the file to the Deputy Minister and prevailed upon him to arrange for a discussion amongst all of us so that a fresh proposal satisfactory to all might be put up before the Chief Minister. Accordingly, a meeting was arranged and efforts were made to approve of the proposals of the Dy. Director Incharge regarding payment to suppliers. But I stuck to my views and told them that if they did not agree with what I had said on the matter they could record their own views and obtain the orders of the Chief Minister. When the file went to the Chief Minister, he agreed entirely with my views. As far as I can remember among other things, the Chief Minister had in his minutes said that the acceptance of these materials, which were of substandard quality and not in keeping with the specifications will put a premium on delinquency and fraud. The order also said that he entirely agreed with the views of the Addl. Director that the materials supplied so far should be rejected, and no payment should be made to the suppliers. The result of this order was that materials worth lacs of Rupees supplied by spurious dealers were rejected and the credibility of the Dy. Director and his associates was greatly shaken. The heads of Institutions who were being pressurised to accept these useless materials heaved a sigh of relief and expressed their gratitude to me for saving them from being a party to the shabby deals.

Soon after this there arose the question of appointing a special officer for the Bhagalpur College of Engineering which was just going to be started. In the previous year when the idea of opening the college had crystallized, the same Deputy Director in the technical education wing was appointed as the special officer in addition to his duties to do the preparatory work for starting the college. This had created a lot of heart-burning amongst senior officers including senior professors of the Engineering colleges, as they all apprehended, and rightly so, that the Dy. Director would eventually become the Principal of the college, superceding their claims. I considered the matter and came to the conclusion that no matter whether the Dy. Directors' appointment as Special Officer meant the supersession of these senior to him or not in the technical sense of the term, this was certainly a backhanded method of promoting nepotism as the Special Officer enjoyed more powers and prestige than even the Principal who was to be appointed in due course. It is interesting to recall that Shri Nageshwar Prasad Singh, the Director of Industries, through whom this file had to pass to Government, came to my room and requested me to put up a proposal for changing the incumbent of the post of Special Officer. Though he himself felt on the same lines, he did not like to thereby offend the Secretary with whom he was on 'first name calling' terms. In my proposal on the subject I dwelt on the inequity of continuing the Dy. Director, a junior officer to this post, and suggested the name of the seniormost Professor in the Engineering Colleges, who as I said could eventually take over as the Principal of the College. This proposal though opposed by the Secretary who pleaded for the continuance of the Dy. Director on the ground that his appointment to this post did not constitute any body's supersession as this post was not in the normal line of their promotion, was approved by the Chief Minister who again commented adversely on having made this inequitous arrangement in the past.

The attitude adopted by me in such matters put a brake to the open loot of the government money and to the atmosphere of rampant favouritism and nepostism which was the order of the day in the Deptt. of Industries and Technical Education. The corrupt and the inefficient became panicky. There were clandestine meetings and conspiracies to make me ineffective by pasting at my back some of the notes recorded by me on government files, I felt sick of the whole atmosphere and decided to leave the Department. Efforts were made also on that side so that I might leave the department soon. Since I found that it was not possible to do any thing substantial in the prevailing atmosphere, I proceeded on leave in April 1962 and was posted as the District Magistrate of Purnea after expiry of my leave in July 1962. Of this, however, I shall speak later.

The above narrative should not lead one to believe that nothing tangible was done during the period of my stay in the Industries Deptt. Even in the Technical Education wing some visible improvements took place. Cases of increments, promotions, sanctions of leave-deputation terms in a number of cases, which had been pending for years, were settled. The Bhagalpur College of Engineering, the junior Technical School, Telaiya and a number of Industrial Training Institutes were set up. The procedure for purchase of equipments was streamlined and a committee of three Dy. Directors was set up to finalise recommendations for purchase of equipments with the assistance of a Principal of a college or a school as the case my be. I also tried in my own way to streamline the working of the powerloom and sericulture sections and it was in recognition of my interest in sericulture that I was elected to the standing committee of the Central Silk Board in the meeting of the Board held at Bombay. This was at the instance of the chairman of the Board who was obviously impressed by my performance in the meeting.

There were, however, certain interesting side-lights which though at times disgusting provided some fun and relief from the daily monotony of life. Though Shri B.N. Sinha, was an efficient officer and could himself write good notes, he employed two ghost writers to write most of his classical notes. One was a classfellow of mine in the college, and the other a friend from school days, (since deceased), both of the Bihar Civil Service, in the rank of Deputy Director. These two officers used to work hard—they collected his views after the daily ritual of discussions and put down everything on behalf of

Sh. B.N. Sinha. This was not all. If any officer recorded a good note on the file, Shri Sinha got his name erased, and the page changed and put up the note as his own to the Minister. The story goes that while he was a Dy. Secretary in the Development Deptt. which then comprised of Industries also, he once pasted a long note of the then Director and submitted the file to the Secretary under his own name. But the Director who had laboured a great deal in preparing this note which was in the nature of a technical project report, had already handed over a copy of this note to the Secretary, a fact which Shri Sinha was not aware of. But those were the heydays of Shri Sinha and no serious notice was taken of it. However, the systematic pasting of good notes of any officer became a standing joke in the Department. Neither I nor Shri N.P. Singh at first believed in it, but once when Shri B.N. Sinha was on a month's leave and Shri N.P. Singh was working in his place and I as Director of Industries, in the place of Shri Singh, Shri N.P. Singh phoned me in a great huff and asked me to come to his room. As soon as I went in, he showed me a file and asked me to read a note. This was a one paged typed note no both sides of the note sheet and I could not readily understand why he should have called me to read this note which did not contain anything extraordinary and bore the signature of Shri B.N. Sinha. On a closer examination I found that a part of the note was pasted with another typed note under which the signature of N.P. Singh was clearly visible. I had a hearty laugh and told Shri Singh that though this happened in his case probably only once, this was the normal practice with Shri B.N. Sinha. I had by then known that some of my notes had also gone to the Minister under the name of Shri Sinha. Not that Shri B.N. Sinha could not write good notes. He was evidently, indulging in this practice to create an impression on the Government that he alone was working hard and doing all the thinking in the Department, and it must be said to his credit that he was to a large extent able to create a myth of being indispensable for the Department.

In all fairness, however, it must mention here that Shri B.N. Sinha in his personal dealings with me and officers generally was a good friend and a considerate boss. Going out with him for meetings outside Patna, particularly to Delhi and other places outside Bihar was a great fun. Mr. Sinha not only looked after us well as his junior colleagues to be taken care of, but often regaled us with interesting stories and jokes in leisure hours. Another good thing about him was that he appreciated good work and respected talent in whomsoever he found. To me and B.R. Gowri Shankar, a Deputy Director looking after Industrial Training Institutes, a person of, unquestionable integrity he was specially good and full of consideration.

4

District Change–The Chinese Aggression

The district of Purnea is situated on the north eastern corner of Bihar having its northern frontier with the Kingdom of Nepal and its eastern part co-terminus with the western boundary of West Bengal. A strip of land, less than ten miles in width, separates it from Bangladesh, then known as East Pakistan. In 1962, the district of Purnea was the gateway to Assam and NEFA. It was the only life line through which flowed the rail and road traffic from the rest of the country to the north eastern region. All civil and military movement to Assam and back had to take place through this district.

When the Chinese army invaded NEFA on the 20th October 1962 the country was not only taken aback, nurtured as the people had been under the euphoria of 'Hindi Chini Bhai Bhai', so assiduously built by our Prime Minister, Jawaharlal Nehru and his cohorts, but was stunned by the crushing defeats suffered successively by our armed forces. Pandit Jawaharlal Nehru was then leaving for Ceylon, and had on being informed of the Chinese advance into the Indian territory confidently asked our Army Chief to throw the Chinese out of India, and the ordinary man in the street thought that the Chinese were going to be taught a lesson for their foolhardy venture. But this was not to be. Battles are not fought with rhetoric alone, and in order that the call of the Political Head of the Government might aid the morale of the armed forces, there must be the wherewithal to fight the enemy with. This was pitifully lacking. The army was poorly equipped, the leadership lacking in ability of effective decision-making and confidence building command, the Air cover was nil and military intelligence was poor. The result : the Chinese army went on storming one defence post after another and the Indian Army lay prostrate until the Chinese reached the very heart of Assam. The marauding band of the Chinese soldiers pushed on without meeting any effective resistance enroute.

The talk of successive defeats by our armed forces reached the nook and corner of the country and the people who had all along been fed with the false belief of the country's security and our brilliant performance on the international plane as propagators and champions of the so called illustrious doctrine of 'panchsheel' felt shocked and let down. The blind faith of the people in the unfailing leadership of Pandit Nehru received a jolt and a sense of resentment and anger overtook them. It became apparent that no serious efforts had been made to augment our armed forces and develop their combat capability. The country was in a state of absolute unpreparedness on the military front. The air force was practically nonexistent in this part of the country. There was no aerodrome in Purnea district and in most parts of the Assam and eastern region. We had no radar equipment, lines of communications were undeveloped; there were several unbridged rivers on the way and crossings had mostly to be effected with the help of country boats. Most roads and even portions of the existing so-called truck roads were unfit to bear the burden of heavy vehicular traffic.

The being the scenario, the Government of India while trying to do whatever could be accomplished on the military and diplomatic fronts took the inevitable decision of evacuating the civilian population from Assam and NEFA in view of the penetrating thrusts of the Chinese army and the near collapse of our armed forces. Since the only route for evacuation both by rail and road lay through the district of Purnea (Katihar being an important Railway Centre) the district became the focal point from which the evacuees could be dispersed in different directions. That being so, the District Magistrate of Purnea became the natural choice for acting as the coordinator for receiving and dispersing the evacuees when actual evacuation started.

A few days after the decision regarding commencement of the evacuation, Shri S.J. Majumdar, Chief Secretary to the Government of Bihar rang me up to inform me about the impending evacuation and asked me to go ahead with the preparation for accommodation, feeding and dispersal of the evacuees to various points in the country from the main rail head at Katihar, as also by road to the extent possible. A large number of I.A.S. officers, mostly young probationers numbering about ten, and a few members of the State Civil Service-Additional District Magistrates and Dy. Collectors drafted from other districts were deputed to assist the District Administration in the gigantic task of tackling the evacuees' problem.

The problem of tackling the refugees when they started pouring in thousands if and when the evacuation was actually ordered, looked quite baffling. Accommodation, food and transport had to be arranged for hundreds of thousands of men, women, and children and care had to be taken to ensure that there was no breakdown in the arrangements. A foolproof system had to be devised.

Immediately after my talk with Chief Secretary I started work on this project. The District Administration had at first to be geared up to face this gigantic task with confidence and efficiency. At a specially convened meeting of all subdivisional officers, concerned District Heads and allied organisations. I explained the gravity of the situation and the crucial role assigned to the district in which we must acquit with credit. The response was intantaneous with faces turned to me with confidence and determination. The SDOs were made squarely responsible for the total arrangements in their respective charge and the officers deputed from outside were placed at strategic points in the district to ensure that nothing went wrong. The State Government deputed an officer of commissioner's rank at Siliguri to keep liaison with the Army authorities. To facilitate. matters, the

Govt. of Indis issued instructions to the Postal authorities to disconnect any telephone and install at any place as and when ordered so by the District Magistrate, on a few hours notice from him so that the flow of refugees when evacuation was actually ordered was not held up resulting in heavy concentration in the District which might inevitably lead to confusion and chaos. The District Magistrate was vested with all powers under the Defence of India Rules. I was supplied with a copy of the War Book. Frequent exercises for decoding of secret messages with their ever changing Code and Key became the order of the day which took a considerable portion of my time. Visits of senior Army and Air Force personnel became a routine with frequent telephonic communications from Delhi and Calcutta Air Headquarters. My telephone was linked with the Army trunk line to facilitate easy communication.

Air Vice Marshal Arjun Singh Dy. Chief of Air Staff visited Purnea to discuss certain secret matters with me and spent a whole day with me. This was followed by the visits of Wing Commander Mehta who was commissioned with the task of selecting a site for an aerodrome at Purnea. When Mehta came down to Purnea we were faced with the difficulty of selecting an appropriate site in the absence of a Helicopter and I had to requast the Burma Oil Company to send a helicopter to help us in our task. And the site on which the Purnea aerodrome now stands was selected by us. A few days later, a coded telegram was received from Air Headquarters that flight Lieutenant Yadav was coming to see me on a secret mission and Yadav arrived the same evening with a big closed an followed by a number of vehicles with uniformed men of the Air Force with a Radar; and the Radar was installed in Purnea town in the premises of a ramshackle building thick with the growth of weeds and tall grass (locally known as Kharaul) having tall trees and bushes which provided a natural camouflage requisitioned by me under the Defence of India rules the following day.

The army authorities maintained day to day contact with me. Brigadier Mohan, Sub area commander, Siliguri was a frequent visitor. Lt. General Candeth who passed through Katihar in the early hours one morning wanted to see me, and a telephonic message was received after midnight to this effect; but the meeting had to be abandoned due to some more urgent matters which cropped up suddenly. In the midst of all these engagements and various other matters requiring my personal attention which kept me busy till past midnight every day, Mr. J.S. Bali, our Liaison officer at Siliguri appeared from time to time to ask me to intercede with the Army authorities to sort out even some minor problems. Brigadier Mohan when confronted told me that their instructions were to deal with the District Magistrate only in all matters. Once when the Commissioner, Bhagalpur Division (under which Purnea District then came) was camping at Purnea, I suggested to the Brigadier who had come to see me to meet the Commissioner, but he politely declined to do so saying that he was not at all concerned with him. Incidentally, I shall not be betraying a trust if I disclose the general attitude of the Army and Air Force officers towards the Police. Air Marshall Arjun Singh had been the first senior officer of the Defence forces to visit Purnea. As soon as he landed he told me that he would like to discuss some secret matters with me preferably at my house. Not knowing how he would take my suggestion when I told him that I would have with me the Superintendent of Police for the discussions, he atonce ejaculated "By God I can not even dream of associating Policemen with such secret discussions. I and you shall be alone and no one else—not even one of my own men (there were ten officers with him including Wing Commander Mehta) will be allowed to be present during our discussions". Later when Flight Lt. Yadav came with the Radar late one evening, and I was confronted with the difficulty of accommodating the vans and a number of vehicles, and I suggested to him whether the vehicles and the men could be kept in the Police lines, he blurted out the same reaction with which I had been confronted with earlier during the visit of Arjun Singh. He did not even agree to send his men to the Police Lines for their meals saying that if any of his men went there the whole thing was bound to leak out, and his specific instructions were not to communicate with the Police in any manner what-so-ever. And the result was that all the vehicles and the men stayed in my compound till they moved to the premises requisitioned for the purpose next day.

In the midst of all these comings and goings there were requests from the Army and Civilian Officers of neighbouring states for various types of assistance. One evening, Mr. Surita, Commissioner of Burdwan division phoned me up from Siliguri and requested me to arrange for about 150 trucks and send them to Siliguri the following morning for transporting troops and supplies to unidentified destinations. Since this was not a direct request from the Army which could be complied with under the Defence of India Rules, I advised him either to request the Army authorities to place a direct requisition or route the request through the Chief Secretary, Bihar, so that an effort could be made to arrange for the trucks. After discussions with the Chief Secretary, who rang me up immediately thereafter, I placed the IAS probationers at different points in the District alongwith some Policemen with instructions to get hold of as many trucks as possible without causing undue hardship to the public; and by 10 'Oclock next morning we were able to collect and despatch 110 trucks to Siliguri full with petrol and providing the drivers with some money for their expenses on the way. I was later told that this was broadcast by All India Radio Delhi in their evening bulletin the same night.

On another occasion, the Chief Secretary of Assam made a direct request to me on the telephone to send him about 30 trucks for transporting tea and we were able to send him 25 or 26 trucks with requests to the Chief Secretary that the truck owners should be paid the hire charges at the prevailing Market rates.

Minor troop movements used to occur by road and the crossing of the convoy across the Ganga at Karhagola used to occupy a good deal of our time and energy. A number of country boats had to be mobilised and the convoys ferried across. The jawans also were invariably entertained to sumptuous meals with the generosity of the local Mukhias under the leadership of the local Sub-divisional Officers and the BDOs. The convoys were also supplied with petrol etc. from the petrol pumps on credit under the standing instructions of the District Magistrate.

Stray officers of the army made their appearance at all odd hours of the day and night. Some had been recalled from leave while others came as an advance party. They came seeking various types of assistance and they were given necessary assistance regarding the topography: routes, and sundry other matters. It was surprising to find that they did not have even the restricted maps to guide them and I had to come to their rescue by showing the maps of the areas which I had under my personal custody.

Movement of army personnel from the front back to their destination was a common phenomenon. They were a pitiable lot, often maimed in the battle, some having frost bites fighting at high altitude without the requisite protective garments, while others suffering from malnutrition aggravated by the inclement condition on the battle front. They were attended to at the railway stations at Purnea and/or Katihar and entertained with tea and snacks. Those in urgent need were provided with pullovers, blankets, socks etc. with the courtesy of the "Ladies of Purnea" a Jawans Welfare club of which my wife, late Srimati Bindhya Vasini Prasad was the President. The members of the club, which was formed soon after the Chinese invaded India, engaged themselves in knitting pullovers, socks, etc and collecting by donation blankets towels, socks and other apparel for the use of Jawans fighting on the front. At a largely attended public meeting held at Kishanganj under the Presidentship of the then Chief Minister, Pandit Binodanand Jha, my wife as the President of the club presented to Brigadier Mohan huge stocks of eatables, large number of knitted wear, blankets, etc. for the benefit of the Jawans.

Purnea being nearest to the front in this state, Civil defence measures on an elaborate scale were introduced. All places of strategic value, air strip, rail and road bridges, petrol pumps situated in out of the way places were guarded by armed police and Homeguard Jawans. Civil Defence personnel were recruited and wardens appointed in each Mahalla. Rifle training camps were organized and the Village Volunteer Force was activised. Exporations for public co-operation and participation in defence efforts were made in small groups and public meetings both by me and by the Ministers coming from Patna from time to time. At one such meeting held in the campus of the Purnea College my speech was tape recorded and later published by the Public Relations Department in the shape of a booklet entitled "Clarion call to the students of Purnea District."

On instructions from the State Government, Collections for the National Defence Fund were started. There was an unprecedented response from the people. Hindus and Muslims, rich and the poor, men, women, and children, all vied with one another in donating for the National Defence Fund whatever they could. Donations in cash, gold and silver ornaments, and sundry articles of value started pouring in and the district established a prominent place in this sphere in the state. It was a moving sight to see the Adivasi Women of a village adjacent to the District Headquarters taking out their few silver ornaments from their person and offering them to the National Defence fund. People seemed to have forgotten all their differences and rallied to the cause to a man. The District Magistrates of five neighbouring districts of West Bengal who had been instructed by their Government to maintain liaison with the District Administration of Purnea were agreeably surprised to see the scale of preparation and activities for the furtherance of defence efforts on their visit to this district.

Side by side with these activities, construction of transit camps for the evacuees if and when they started pouring in, was taken in hand under the personal supervision of the sub-divisional officers concerned. These centres were chosen for establishing transit camps the one at Kishanganj the second at Purnea and the third at Karhagala—a place on the bank of Ganga near Katihar, from where people could be ferried across the Ganga in country boats and sent to various points by rail or road. The three transit camps which were built with bamboo and straw could conveniently hold amongst themselves 60,000 persons at any point of time. These camps which were built in the record time of a week were constructed entirely out of voluntary donations and free labour, the amount spent out of public exchequer being limited to Rs. 27 only. Even the expenditure of this small sum was necessitated because one night at Kishanganj the winding rope ran short and a shop had to be opened late at night from which rope for this amount had to be purchased so that the construction work could continue uninterrupted. I still remember that S.K. Lal the SDO rang me up at about 10-00 PM and regretfully told me that the work would have to be stopped because the stock of rope had run short, and I had to cheer him up saying that if he was so keen to complete the work by the morning he could purcha.e the required quantity of rope from the market by getting a shop opened. This single incident is characteristic of the sense of dedication and urgency with which the officials of the District took their work during these trying times. And this effort on the part of the administration in the construction of three massive camps in record time at a total cost of Rupees Twenty Seven to the Public Exchequer was broadcast by the All India Radio in their evening bulletin at 9-00 PM a couple of days later.

The three transit camps at Kishanganj, Purnea Karhagala were provided with the minimum basic necessities. Letrines and bathrooms (for women only) were constructed in each camp separately for men and women, street lighting was done with wooden electric poles put up at vantage points in the colony. Street hydrants were provided to ensure adequate water supply. A police chowki was opened in each camp for maintenance of peace and public order. Grains, vegetables, kerosene oil, salt etc. were arranged in each subdivision to be brought to the camps at short notice. The stocks of rice were frozen with rice mills in Kishanganj, Katihar and Araria subdivision for use of the refugees under the Defence of India rules.

Public health measures were also taken care of. Separate sheds for kitchen were built and kachha drains were laid out linking the kitchen, the bathing place and the street hydrants along broad pathways which were laid down between two sets of hutments throughout the colony. Sufficient quantity of bleaching powder disinfectants and first aid boxes were stocked for use in the camps. An IAS officer was placed in charge of each camp under the overall supervision of the sub-divisional officer who had to be constantly in touch with me.

During the course of all these feverish activities a difference of opinion arose between me and the Supply Department over the food that was to be supplied to the refugees. The Supply Department through their Dy. Secretary, Shri Anjani Kumar Verma sent me a message that the refugees should be fed with chapaties as this would be cheaper than feeding them with rice. I told him that this was an unworkable proposition because it would be well nigh impossible to cope with the situation as and when the refugees started pouring in thousands, and added that I intended to make arrangements for supply of cooked rice as and when the arrivals started. This decision of mine necessitating the freezing of rice in the Rice Mills of the district came in handy to the Commissioner of Bhagalpur division who for no ostensible reason, did not take kindly to the magnificent Defence efforts which the district administration was making under my supervision. However, his efforts to put me in trouble did not find support with the State Government. Incidentally, the rice which was reserved in the mills was sold at a higher price than what we had paid for, after I had left the District.

While all these arrangements had been completed and the administration and the people of Purnea were well set to receive the evacuees and disperse them in different directions by rail and road, the Chinese declared a unilateral ceasefire on 21.11.62, one month after the commencement of hostilities, and so the movement of multitude of refugees did not take place. Though we all felt a sigh of relief, the colossal efforts made by us in putting up these transit camps passed off as an exercise in futility. But we had the satisfaction of having put through the whole scheme within minimum time with almost no cost to Government. All this was largely due to the implicit obedience, ungrudging assistance and co-operation on the part of the subdivisional officers—Sarbashri S.K. Lal of

Kishanganj and Sitaram Gope of Katihar, and the officer working under them. Pandit Binodanand Jha, Chief Minister of Bihar who later visited Purnea was highly struck by the colossal efforts put in by the administration in building these huge complexes and for making such elaborate and detailed arrangements for tackling the expected evacuation of civilians from Assam and NEFA. This, as stated above, fortunately did not take place.

The elaborate arrangements made for tackling the refugee problem, the District Emergency scheme, the civil defence measures, the incessant visits of high military officers and the confidence and respect with which I was treated by them excited the jealousy of my Commissioner, Shri K. Abraham, an Ex-Army man who got into the IAS after demobilisation. For reasons that I could not fathom then, Shri Ab-aham did not take kindly to the efforts being made by us for assisting in the defence of the country. Shri Abraham had been the collector of Purnea in 1950 and though his knowledge of the District was very much out of date he always tried to interfere in any arrangement which was being made, and often adopted an obstructionist attitude during one of which he was openly cold shouldered by the Brigadier. Mr. Abraham and I had different outlook on many matters. While he could take recourse to any contrivance to put into trouble those that he did not like and conversely to benefit those whom he liked, I always tried to take an objective view of things, an attitude which was not looked upon with approbation in the then existing administrative climate in Bihar which has been the bane of the Bihar administration all through the years. Soon after I joined at Purnea I was told that my predecessor, R.N. Mitra under the dictates of Mr. Abraham had written to the Government for the reversion of the SDO of Katihar, Sitaram Gope, obviously because he had issued a notice of contempt against the Deputy Superintendent of Police, a blue eyed boy of the commissioner, for his persistent refusal to appear in the court in connection with a criminal case, which the officers of Purnea who met me in a body resented very much. Since all this had happened before I joined the District, I could do nothing in this regard, and the matter was allowed to rest at that. But the Government decided that the opinion of the new District Magistrate should also be obtained as the punishment suggested by my predecessor to which the Commissioner had simply concurred appeared to be too drastic, as Gope had done another subdivision with credit and had a uniformly good record of service. Mr. Abraham who evidently had come to know of this had during my first meeting with him at Bhagalpur at which the Collector of Monghyr and other districts of the Division were also present broached this subject, and virtually asked me to say the same thing about Gope as my predecessor had said. The Government did not call for any report from me officially but I came to know that the Chief Minister who was scheduled to visit Purnea shortly would ask for my views in the matter. I, therefore, looked into the whole case in detail and came to the conclusion that the SDO was not at fault and the report sent against him was unfair. Nevertheless, I sent for the SDO and the Deputy Superintendent of Police and asked them to make up. The only way, to my mind, was that the Dy. SP would appear in the court and the SDO would drop the matter. Even though they did what I had told them to do, the DSP evidently felt let down and told the Commissioner about it. However, when the Chief Minister visited the district and enquired from me about Sitaram Gope, I gave him my views in the matter. This was the end of Sitaram Gope's affair and he continued as the SDO of Katihar. When Abraham came to know about it he became furious and openly expressed his displeasure to me.

Mr. Abraham was an 'eat, drink and be merry type', of a man. He was on very intimate terms with the big landlord of Kursela Babu Raghubans Prasad Singh. Shri Abraham and the Kursela Babus were family friends and quite often on Saturdays or Sundays Mr. Abraham's family flew to Kursela in the Kursela plane to spend the weeknd with them. He was naturally very soft towards them, and when under government orders I asked the SDO Katihar to but the Karhagola ghat to auction, as a departure from the past as the Kursela

Raj as it was known in the district, always got the settlement of the ghat on a mere pittance, Mr. Abraham was visibly annoyed but could not do much in the matter. However, Babu Raghubans Prasad Singh got the ghat even that year though Raghubans Babu had to shell out 15% more than the normal amount. This only meant a reduction of about Rs. 25,000 in his income from the ghat as the ghat in the past was let out by him at twice or thrice the amount that he paid to the government.

Raja P.C. Lal of Purnea, a venerable old man of a really aristocratic family was the other person with whom Mr. Abraham was on very friendly terms. He freely enjoyed his hospitality and went out of the way to help him even at the cost of Govt. revenue. Purnea had a large number of melas almost throughout the year. Gulab bagh mela which was held just in Purnea town used to be settled with the Raja. Since no bidder would come up for the Mela ground settlement in deference to Raja P.C. Lal, that year we decided to hold the mela departmentally, and with the zeal and hard work put in by the revenue officials, the mela was a thumping success and we collected more money for the Government than the Raja ever paid to the past. Once during my time when Abraham went to lunch with the Raja, he reversed an order passed by his predecessor, Dr. G. Jacob which resulted in some unlawful gain to the Raja. I protested about the Commissioner's action but, as usual nothing happened.

As indicated earlier, Mr. Abraham's visits to Purnea did not always relate much to any Government work. Once in the dead of night when the situation on the military front was precarious and the whole Governmental machinery was engaged busy preparing plans for the next day, I had a telephonic communication regarding General Candeth's visit to Purnea on way to NEFA in the early hours of the following morning, Shri Abraham was then spending the night in the house of Babu Raghubans Prasad Singh at Kursela and I had to speak to him on the telephone at an unearthly hour because the Superintendeat of Police, Rameshwar Lal who was very close to Abraham was also spending the night at Kursela. I asked the Commissioner to send the S. P. to Katihar to escort the General to Purnea. However, the General's visit to Purnea had to be cancelled as he took the train at Katihar itself due to some emergent circumstance.

The babus of Kursela unlike Raja P. C. Lal who came of an old aristocratic family and had the hereditary title of Raja bestowed upon them by the British Government, were a new rich people. The family wielded considerable influence both among Government Servants and at the political level. There was a spate of parties given by them at Kursela. Shri Raghubans Prasad Singh's modus operandi was to cultivate important officers at the District, Divisional and State levels, besides building good rapport with Ministers and others of consequence by throwing lavish parties in their honour at which he always made it a point to invite the important officials of the District. Soon after, I had joined he came to see at Purnea and requested me to have a meal at Kursela with him. But, I politely declined his invitation. His greatest regret was that he was unable to persuade me even to join any party at his house given in honour of dignitories coming from outside. I had made it a point not to accept or join any private party in my official capacity and I stuck to this principle scrupulously as long as I was posted in Araria or Purnea or even at Chaibasa in particular, and throughout my official career generally. Raghubans Babu must have been greatly disappointed when I did not accompany the Governor of Bihar who had accepted Raghubans Babu's invitation for lunch at Kursela. The Governor on hearing my plea about my principle of not accepting any private hospitality had been gracious enough to permit me to stay back and depute the ADM to accompany him. When Shri Jagjiwan Ram also went to Kursela for lunch and I accompanied him at his insistence, I excused myself from joining the lunch on the pretext that the particular day was the one on which I abstained from food till sunset.

Soon after my posting at Purnea, my relations with the Commissioner underwent a strain in connexion with the case of Sitaram Gope, SDO of Katihar, as discussed earlier. The incident regarding the Kursela family, Raja P.C. Lal's affair, the unkindly attitude adopted by him to my efforts in connection with the Chinese invasion of NEFA witnessed a sharpening of my differences with Mr. Abraham. The then Speaker of the Bihar Assembly, Dr. Lakshmi Narayan Sudhanshu, also a resident of this district, was not too happy with me due to my attitude towards the Kursela family who were his kinsmen. A whispering campaign was started for my transfer which took the shape of a clamour towards the end of December, 1962. Soon after the Chinese danger abated. Mr. Abraham who was favourably disposed towards vested interests of the district, remonstrated with Dr. Sudhanshu to put political pressure on the Chief Minister for my transfer. The bogey of my promoting leftist activities by the due support to the Sikmidars and the Bataidars, most of whom were Adivasis-Santhals, was raised in pseudo-anonymous petitions and petitions containing forged signatures engineered by the Commissioner's henchmen, and openly blessed by him, were sent to the authorities. This was primarily due to my visiting the place of occurrence where an adivasi Bataidar was murdered, obviously at the instance of the landlord, a kinsman of Dr. Sudhanshu who was a silent leader of the landlords who took recourse to a saulting, intimidating and even physically eliminating such persons who asked for their due share in the produce according to the law. Readers might recall that it was the same Dr. Sudhanshu who was involved in the multiple murder of share croppers in Purnea year later and who was charge-sheeted as one of the principal accused, and died during the pendency of the trial. I had in one of my letters hinted at Dr. Sudhanshu's involvement in such matters before, and P.S. Appu who became the Commissioner of Kosi division later came to see me at Patna and expressed his surprise as to how I could make such a forecast. Ironically, such men occupied such high offices in this state. During the Chief Minister's visit to purnea in December 1962, one such petition was submitted to the Chief Minister in the Circuit House containing certain allegations regarding my instigating the Adivasis to harvest the crop force fully. The Chief Minister handed over the petition to me and asked me to apprise him with the facts of the matter in due course. One of the so-called signatories came to me a few days later in connexion with the renewal of his pistol or revolver licence. When casually asked, with a view to ascertaining the facts, whether he had signed on the petition, he asserted that he had never even come across this petition. The man was examined on oath by the Public Prosecutor in the open court who asserted that he had nothing to do in the matter and that his signature had been clearly forged. A report was sent to the Government and those who had sponsored this forged document stood fully exposed.

The discredited Congress leadership who had also some grouse against me for my refusal to go to the congress office and join in the flag hoisting ceremony there on the 15th August, as my two predecessors Shri S K. Chakravorty and Shri R.N. Mitra did, were also goaded by the commissioner through his henchmen, to join in the clamour for my transfer. The Chief Minister who had a high opinion of my work and ability did not at first agree to this preposterous demand. But he surrendered to the pressure of the political forces led by Dr. Lakshmi Narayan Sudhansu and my transfer was decided in January 1963; and I made over my office on 29.1. 63.

My transfer from Purnea was an affront to the people particularly the poor Adivasis and the landless Bataidars. The Adivasis raised a demonstration in the Circuit House before the Governor who visited Purnea towards the end of my stay there when the transfer order had already been received. The Governor, Sh. Ananta Shayanam Ayyangar, whom I knew from before, expressed a desire to visit my house probably to express his appreciation for my work and the authorities were told about it. Route lining by the police had been done and my wife had made arrangements to receive the Governor and his wife properly. When Dr. Lakshmi Narayan Sudhanshu came to know about it he ran to the Governor and persuaded him not to visit my house and the Governor had willy-nilly to cancel the visit at the last moment. He personally rang me up and told me that since the Speaker objected to his visit he had decided not to proceed with it. But he made up by sending his wife to meet us at our house and we have some photographs of hers with my family members. The Chief Minister who had visited Purnea earlier also made it up by inviting me and my wife along with our son Ashok to lunch with him at Purnea Circuit House to the exclusion of the Commissioner and the DIG of Police who were also camping with him in the Circuit House itself.

My transfer from Purnea was a memorable event and has left a vivid impression on my mind. The officers and staff of Purnea collectorate and allied offices, the Purnea club 'T' club, and the officers and staff of various other offices gave farewell parties. I still recall an interesting incident which happened on the night the officers of Purnea had met to bid me farewell at a dinner given by them. The Chief Minister was also camping at Purnea that night and wanted to participate in the Dinner. The Speaker who also happened to be at Purnea that day got a scent of it and had proposed that the Chief Minister dine with him. The Chief Minister who was thoroughly annoyed by the goings on at Purnea under Shri Sudhanshu's inspiration decided not to oblige him and the moment he came to talk to him about it he feighed illness and confined himself to the bed room. The Civil Surgeon was called and he declared that the CM should not see any visitors. Sudhanshuji waited for hours but the Chief Minister did not come out and eventually he with his henchmen went back with a wry face. Later that evening the C.M. desired that he must at least partake of the food to be served at my dinner, and a basket load of food was transferred to the Circuit House which the C.M. ate with relish, before I joined the officers at the dinner hosted by them in my honour.

These are no doubt, memorable events. But the farewell which I got at the Purnea Railway Station has been the most touching event in my life. Thousands of people led by Adivasis with drums, conchshells and their traditional musical instruments moved in a procession and thronged the railway station and literally covered me with garlands. They had spread red cloth at the platform and vocal and instrumental music interspersed with 'jais' marked the departure of the collector who was transferred when he was trying to put the district administration on a clean footing by eliminating corruption, nepotism and exploitation of the poor by the rich. The police, however, under instructions of the S.P., Shri Rameshwer Lal, Yesman of the Commissioner kept aloof. The armed force stationed at my Bungalow wanted to accompany me to the Railway Station but I discouraged them as this might be construed as ostentatious display of pomp and pageantry.

A few interesting episodes need to be related. During the visit of the Chief Minister to Purnea on the eve of my departure, he had made a programme, at my instance, to visit a Panchayat situated in a remote area. The Commissioner who always took an opposite view to any of my proposals, tried to persuade the Chief Minister not to visit the place. But the Chief Minister stuck to his programme. Since the place was accessible from the Assam access Road between Siliguri and Kishanganj, we flew to Bagdogra Airport in West Bengal and thereafter we were to motor down to the place. The commissioner who had reached the Dak Bungalow earlier, from where the party was to proceed to the village threw the final trumpcard and told the Chief Minister that since a bridge on the way was unsafe he would not like the Chief Minister and the Speaker to undertake the journey. But as I had visited the place only a few days earlier and had passed through the bridge which had only the side railings broken, I told the Chief Minister that the bridge was safe enough and there was no danger in going. When the Chief Minister accompanied by the Speaker, myself and the SP passed through the bridge, the Chief Minister jocularly remarked to the speaker in Maithili "Are we bullocks that we would stray aside and fall in the ditch ?" Haman Ki Bail theka je bharak kegir parab. The villagers who were present in thousands lustily cheered the Chief Minister and the function was a great success.

Since it had become dark, we started back to Kishanganj by bar. The Superintendent of Police and some others followed in another vehicle. A very interesting thing happened on the way. The CM expressed his desire that he wanted to make water. Pandit Binodanand Jha who was an extremely bulky man, could not sit down to make water due to his bulk, and somebody had to assist him to stand erect for this purpose. I jocularly suggested to the SP to hold his Dhotee on one side so that the poor old fellow could make water without spilling urine on his Dhotee. It was a funny sight seeing the SP holding the Dhotee of the CM and the latter making water without concern.

Towards the beginning of January 1963, I went out on a tour of the border areas in Kishanganj sub-division falling on this side of Nepal. I along with the SDO Kishanganj, S.K. Lal, and the Asstt. Superintendent of Police, Krit Bhu Deo set out on the two-day marathon tour and covered all the areas on the long border, during some times till midnight, on the dusty forsaken road. It was so satisfying to see the jawans keeping vigil on these far flung areas cut off from all vistas of civilisation.

One night we reached a place probably called Bandar Jhula, if I remember the name right. There was an Anchal Kacheri where officers generally stayed. But I preferred to stay in the Dak Bungalow nearby. The SDO tried to persuade me not to stay at this abandoned place; but ultimately on my persuasion we moved in there. This was a very old Dak Bungalow. There were two rooms besides a small dinning room. I slept in one and the SDO and Assistant Superintendent of Police shared the other room between them. In the middle of the night, there was a bang and when I opened my eyes I found that I was lying on the floor. I called the SDO but he was fast asleep, but the ASP rushed to my room with the revolver in his hand sensing some trouble. When the SDO and others got up the SDO said that this was a hunted place and that is why he had objected to our staying there. What had actually happened was that when the cots were arranged, an old cot with top from another one which had disappeared in course of time was placed for me, in great hurry, and the same slipped and I fell on the ground when I might have changed side. We had all a hearty laugh in the morning. The visitors book disclosed that the last to stay in the Dak Bungalow was a British Collector in 1932.

This tour between the 3rd and 6th of January 1963 which covered the entire subdivision was monumental for the amount of work that was done from Revenue, Law and Order, Medical, Civil, Defence to welfare and Plan Project. The comprehensive tour note recorded by me which must be lying in the Collectorate is self revealing.

Soon after I left Purnea, I got two small booklets published by the officers and Staff of Purnea. One of these contained the address which I had given to the students of Purnea college as a part of the Civil Defence drive and the other an embarrassing publication containing eulogies bestowed on me on the eve of my transfer.

5

Survey and Settlement—District Singhbhum

I joined my new post as Settlement Officer of Singhbum District at Chaibasa in the first week of February 1963. The post of a Settlement Officer was a prized post during the British days and very senior and upcoming officers used to be given this assignment. The British Government was interested in revenue administration for obvious reasons. The settlement Reports written by them are still considered the last word on the question of land tenures, fixation of fair rent and portrayal of the State of Peasantry of the contemporary period. But the past has now been relegated to the background as has happened also with the Member, Board of Revenue, and inconvenient and some times inefficient officers are now shoved into these posts. But the old paraphernalias still remain and the Settlement officer is still the absolute Monarch of all he surveys.

When I joined at Chaibasa, the survey fieldwork had nearly been completed and preparation of final records and their distribution was just in hand. The job of a Settlement Officer is not considered so important as it used to be in the past. Even so, I toured extensively and saw almost the whole of the district. A study of Adivasi life was particularly fascinating. The Adivasis who had been deprived of their lands due to the machinations of Amins and the antipathy of officers were during my time given their due by the Settlement Officer in the shape of court decrees and hundreds of settlement entries were corrected in their favour. Official life was otherwise dull, drab und monotonous with nothing exciting to demand original thinking in the normal course of work. The one good result of my posting was that I prepared the Settlement Report of the Singhbhum settlement (1958-65) which was later published by the Government and was favourably received. This was the first report on Settlement operations that was written since Independence in Bihar. This is a voluminous documeut containing countless statistics and numerous maps which throw a vivid light on the working not only of the land revenue administration of the district but also the irrigation projects, the growth centres like hats, ghats, bazaars, etc., the railways and the roads besides the physical features. hill ranges, rivers, rainfall, climate etc. The preparation of the report took a lot of time and the report could be completed much after my leaving Chaibasa and published only in 1970. The book also contains chapters on the social, cultural and economic life of the "HOs", "Santhals", "Mundas", besides the Bhuinyas of Singhbhum—a group entirely forgotton in the previous narratives. The account of the Bhuinyas is based on a palm leaf manuscript written in Oriya dating back to more than 150-200 years. This account of the Bhuinyas was also published in the journal of the Bihar Research Society which also published hundreds of copies of it in the shape of a small book for distribution among the members and others interested in research projects. The following extracts from the Settlement Report of Singhbhum (1958-65) throw light on the Bhuinyas of Singhbhum :

> "There are a large number of Bhuinyas settlements on the border of Kolhan around Seraikella, Kharsawan area, Jayantgarh, Jaganathpur, Porhat and Chandil. Though physically separated, the inhabitants of these areas share their belief and tradition in common, inter-marry and worship in the same fashion. Since their members are small and since no efforts were made to study them separately as a class, no special notice of this community was taken before. However, during the period of my stay in Singhbhum, wherever I went, I heard a story of their common ancestors and of their distinct entity. from the

older persons of that community. I also heard that the Bhuinyas ruled over most parts of this district and that their last ruler lived at a place on the bank of the Sanjaya. I was able to locate this place and talk to their leaders. A manuscript written on palm leaves containing an account of their migration and history was given to me. The manuscript is written in Oriya language."

"From a reading of that book, it appears that the Bhuinyas of Singhbhum originally belonged to a place known as "Bhuj" on the western side of Bhopal. They were originally Kshatriyas, but due to some social upheavals and political and economic reasons they had to migrate to this place. The central theme of the book revolves round one Raja Narangi who happened to be the Raja of Bhuj. It is difficult to ascertain when this Raja Narangi actually lived and when did this migration take place."

"But the story as unfolded by the manuscript throws distinct light on certain social and religious customs which are still prevalent among the Bhuinyas of Singhbhum. For instance, even today when a new King is to be crowned in Seraikella or Keonjhar, a Bhuinyan Chief has to offer the crown to the ruler, a custom which finds mention in the manuscript. The book also explains the origin of the names of certain places in the district of Singhbhum."

Another interesting find was a thousand year old copper plates.

It was a strange coincidence that when on a particular day I was about to leave for inspection of a camp court near Kharsawan, an employee of the camp who had come to Chaibasa, met me and casually mentioned to me that an old copper plate had been found by someone who was reported to have said that he wanted to present the same to me. Though I was sceptical about the information I went for my inspection and after completing the work went out to the market along with the Assistant Settlement Officer and some of his staff. While we were about to turn back, the same person who had met me at Chaibasa suddenly pointed out towards and old gentlemen coming from the opposite direction and said that this was the person who was reported to have the copper plate. On being asked as to where he was going, the old man said that he was going towards the camp site to take a chance of meeting the Settlement Officer who, as he heard, was to come there on that day. I disclosed my identity and came to the inspection bungalow with him and others in my car. On being asked if he had any problem in connection with the Settlement Operations he said that he had none but added that he wanted to have a few words with me in private without anyone else being present there. And as soon as all others had left the room, he brought out an object wrapped in a newspaper and handed it over to me saying that this was the Copper Plate which he had decided to give to me. He also requested me not to divulge his name to anybody as the local Raja who had heard about the Copper Plate had been pressing him to give it to him; but he had flatly denied any knowledge about the Copper Plate as he apprehended that if the Raja got it he might sell it to a foreigner. He further added that he had decided to give it to me because he had heard that I was interested in things of antiquity and was convinced that this valuable thing would be put to proper use by me. He left thereafter bearing with smile.

The Copper Plate contains inscriptions in the local language prevalent in this part of the country dating back to the year 1081 Bikram era corresponding to 1024-25 A.D. It contains writings in Sanskrit partly in press and partly in verse in the local Devanagri script of the 11th Century A.D. The inscriptions records the grant of village Simvala situated in Vishaya District of Subsrnakhada by Maharaja Dhiraj Kram Dwitya Dev to one Purushottama Devi, son of Bhatta Upatto who had migrated from Kasatay. Judging by their title, Prachand Ditya and Kramaditya appearing in the inscription appear to have been independent kings, but they are not known to History so far. The identification of these kings must be left to future research.

The Copper Plate was found near the bank of river Sanjay about four miles from Kharsawan near the site of village Ramgarh. A photo copy of the Copper Plate appears on the following page.

My labour was rewarded when Government approved of all my recommendations and the foreword published along with the book commended me for the good work done and the useful report. They also sanctioned a special remuneration for the writing of the report.

The period of my stay at Chaibasa was, however, quite pleasant at the social level. Because of my seniority and also because of my wide social contacts I was treated with great consideration and respect not only by the officials but also by the general public. We had put up an extremely beautiful garden in our house which attracted a large number of visitors. The Dy. Commissioner Shri J.P. Srivastava, an extremely gentle patriarchal figure, the Superintendent of Police, Haroon Rashid and the officers of the forest department all clustered around my house which had become more or less a social club. During festival times, Holi, Dewali and Dussehra in particular, there used to be a stream of visitors and we sometimes found it difficult to look after the crowd. The forest department was particularly obliged to me for I had given them the Dalma Forest Range which had been recorded in the name of the Tata Iron & Steel Company due to the connivance of the lower staff. When this came to my notice at the time of final preparation of the 'Record of Rights', I *suo moto* started proceedings and cancelled the entries after giving the Tata Iron & Steel Company and the Forest Department a formal hearing in my court. In the beginning the local officials of the forest department seemed lukewarm but later when I issued a notice to the Chief Conservator of Forests they woke up to their responsibilities. Eventually, however, the Hon'ble Supreme Court of India negatived the order on some technical flaw in the order of the Board of Revenue which on appeal had confirmed my order, but had introduced certain extraneous matter in the judgement.

When Shri K.B. Sahay became the Chief Minister after

Pandit Binodanand Jha had been axed under the Kamraj plan and visited Chaibasa, the local people, it seems, spoke a great deal about me and he told some of them who later confided to me that I would take over as the Dy. Commissioner of Singhbhum after the departure of Shri J.P. Srivastava who was soon to leave. But his powerful colleague in the Cabinet, it was rumoured, had his way and Shri Harbans Narayan Singh, a promoted Officer, succeeded Shri Srivastava. Harbans Narayan Singh was far junior to me in service, but we had quite a happy relationship between us.

6

Public Relations—The First United Front Government and the Bihar Famine

Soon thereafter, I was transferred to Patna and joined as Director of Public Relations Bihar, on 31 March, 1965 and continued for quite some time. This was a period of stress and strain. Shri K.B. Sahay and his cabinet colleagues had become quite unpopular towards the end of their term and the PRD had a difficult time defending the Government.

The Public Relations Department had been rendered more or less defunct. The Department was being utilised by the Ministers for their personal work. PRD photographers were utilised during private functions in Ministers' families like marriages, parties and the like. The climax of it was that during the Khatna (Circumcision) ceremony of a grand son of the then State Minister for Information and Public Relations, the PRD photographers were stated to have taken pictures of the actual ceremony. The film section, likewise, was also being misused in a similar fashion. These extraneous demands on the staff left them little time to do any useful work. This was also possible because a large number of officers of the PRD were generally drawn from ranks of workers of the Congress party who were rewarded with these assignments after the congress came to power in the wake of independence.

While I was still groping my way to put the organisation on a proper keel, the then Information Minister, Smt. Sumitra Devi told me only a week or ten days after my joining that the Prime Minister, Shri Lal Bahadur Shastri had agreed to perform the opening ceremony of the proposed Bihar Information Centre at Delhi and that 27 April had been fixed as the date for the opening ceremony. I was simply aghast as when I looked at the file I found that even the scheme for opening opening an Information Centre at Delhi had not yet been sanctioned by the Government. Sanction of a scheme of this nature is not generally cleared by the Finance Department quickly, because such schemes entail both recurring and non-recurring expenditure. However, since this was a useful scheme and the Prime Minister had agreed to inaugurate it on 26.4.65, I plunged myself whole heartedly in the affair. I drafted a scheme, got it cleared by the Finance Department by having a discussion with the Finance Secretary and took the file personally to the Chief Minister, who at first grumbled at the way the matter was being hustled through even without his knowledge; but when I explained the implications of not getting through the scheme he approved the proposal and sanctioned its implementation in anticipation of the approval of the Council of Ministers. Since I was able to get the entire thing cleared in only one day, I felt greatly reassured and set myself to the task of making the function a great success. I visited Delhi a couple of times, had the building, the Mandi House done up tastefully, selected the furniture, fixtures, curtains, durries etc. and arranged for a big function and a garden party on the occasion at which the Chief Minister naturally had to play the Chief host. At Patna, I personally dictated a brochure on 'Bihar' in English and this along with its Hindi version was published in two separate brochures. This publication which was distributed in the function depicted the saga of Bihar through the ages right from the dawn of history and upto the modern times, was greatly liked for its contents and fine get-up and high order of printing, Shri S.N. Chatterjee, Superintendent of the Government Printing Press, Patna and Shri Akshaya Kumar Sinha, now deceased, a Dy. Director in the PRD who made the Hindi rendering of the book, deserve all praise for their efforts.

The Pandal where the function was held was tastefully decorated with myriads of lights and flower pots and the Prime Minister gave a homely and illuminating speech while inaugurating the function in which the Chief Minister, Shri K.B. Sahay and Information Minister were also present.

Soon after, a piquant situation arose over the question of providing PA sets (Public Address sets) for a political conference of the Indian National Congress to be addressed by Smt. Indira Gandhi, the then Information Minister in the Government of India, at Hazaribagh. Since the prevalent practice had been for the PRD to cover all such functions, a routine order in the mater was communicated by the Chief Secretary, I argued that while the PRD could depute their photographers who could take the photographs and send them to the Press, it would not be proper for the PRD to provide PA sets for the conference of a political party, because if we dip this in one case we could not refuse a similar request by other political parties. Nobody, however, was prepared to pass orders. When I met the Chief Secretary, Shri T.P. Singh, ICS and explained my viewpoint he immediately saw the force behind my reasoning and put up the file to the Chief Minister advising acceptance of my proposal. The Chief Minister agreed with my views and the embarassing situation was averted.

Chief Minister K.B. Sahay was too well known in politics to require a significant space in this narrative. He was a bold, courageous and forthright person. He believed firmly in his principles and though he was generally known to stick to his own views, he was always amenable to reasonable suggestions and often took decisions against his known predilections with good grace. He had, however, a rough tongue and he could give a forth right 'NO' even to those who mattered a great deal in public life. He was the ablest administrator that we have had among the politicians and his minutes written in English were a literary treat. To my mind he was a person more sinned against than sinning. Most of the canards against him were started by those whom he maintained not only politically but also financially throughout their lives. I have had the good fortune of knowing him intimately during the term of my posting in the PRD and can safely assert that when he could be convinced with reason he did not hesitate to resile from the stand taken by him.

The Chief Minister once got interested in a small case of grant of annual contract for the printing of an Urdu monthly brought out by the PRD "Bihar Ki Khabaren." He mentioned this to me and wanted the contract to be awarded to a certain person who had approached him. As the quotation of this gentleman was higher than that of some other persons I had decided to award the work to the lowest tenderer. When I started explaining the matter he got impatient and wanted that the file should be put up to him so that he could himself pass orders in the matter. I went back to the office and when I returned to him with the file, I requested him to give me a hearing before passing orders in the matter. When I explained to him that it would be improper for the Chief Minister to award the contract to a person whose tender rates were higher than the one I proposed to award, he immediately saw my point and asked me to take back the file and do whatever I considered proper in the matter.

Shri K.B. Sahay was known as a disciplinarian and a person who could not tolerate a mistake. Soon after I joined, probably during the Budget session of the Bihar Legislature, an unfortunate incident took place. The Chief Minister sent me an extract of a speech delivered in the Assembly for publication in shape of a pamphlet and '*dissribution broadcast*'. I did not have a close look at it and passed it on to the Dy. Director of publications. All, including me, thought that this was K.B. Sahay's speech, though it was that of the Speaker, and as such the speech was published in the Chief Minister's name. Overnight and 50,000 copies of the same at that. Next day, early in the morning the mistake was detected at the instance of a press representative and I felt a sense of utter shame and failure on my part. However, I immediately got all the copies under my charge, sealed them and kept them in the almirah, deputed the Deputy Director with a special request to the Superintendent of the Government Press, who was a good friend of mine, to print 50000 copies in the name of Speaker at once and bring as many thousand of copies as possible by 11 AM when the Assembly was to meet. As soon as the Assembly met the Speaker at the instance of some of the members drew the attention of the Chief Minister to this mistake. The Chief Minister became furious and I was summoned to his room in the Assembly. When I met him I immediately owned the mistake and expressed great regret for the same which I pleaded with him had been made in good faith. I also told him about the corrective steps that had been taken an showed him some copies of the freshly published document. To the astonishment of all, the Chief Minister immediately felt mollified and asked me to meet the Speaker and express my regret for it which I did immediately by going to the Speaker's chamber. The Information Minister Smt. Sumitra Devi who had not taken kindly to my posting in the Department as she wanted to continue the old incumbent, a Departmental candidate, Shri Mahi Narayan Jha who had turned out to be so obliging and convenient to her and was jubiliant that I was going to get a bang was sorely disappointed at the considerate attitude shown by the Chief Minister.

The term of my posting in the PRD witnessed many interesting incidents and some unpleasant ones too. The PRD, as indicated earlier, consisted of officers recruited at different points of time without any set rules and qualifications at the beginning of the post-Independence era, and was a dumping ground for the favourites of Ministers. The officers of the PRD were pseudo-politicians and quite a few of them were a *useless lot*. The Addl. Director, Shri Mahi Narayan Jha who had risen from the ranks could go to the farthest limits to please any politician, more so the Minister. He had officiated for wellover eight months as the Director of the Department prior to my joining that post. It was his great ambition to become the permanent Director of the Department and with this end in view, he would start a whispering campaign against any Director and would create all conceivable obstacles in the proper functioning of the Department. Though Mahi Narayan Jha was not bad in his dealings with me as according to him he and I had been class fellows—a fact which I do not recollect even now—he was subtly trying to create conditions so that nothing tangible was done. His *modus operandi* was to block action in any field and to point out to the Minister in small talks that nothing tangible could happen in the Department. The day I joined the Department, Mahi Narayan Jha proceeded on four months' leave and during this period, a lot of uselful work was done. But soon after he returned from leave he started putting obstacles in the way. But there were [some good and efficient persons too. Shri Akshaya Kumar Sinha the Deputy Director of Periodicals Shri Surendra Bahadur, the Dy. Director of Publications, Shri Mahe Munir Khan, Deputy Director, Press, ably assisted by Satya Ranjan Bihari Sahay and Goverdhan Prasad 'Saday' were of immense assistance in managing and improving upon the publications cf books and periodicals, issue of press hand-outs etc. Others [who deserve mention were Sorbashri N.P. Sinha (Nareshji). Bhubneshwar Dwivedi and P C. Chatterjee all Dy. Derectors, Akshaya Babu was good Hindi writer and was the Chief Editor of the PRD publications, like the Bhiar Information Bihar Samachar and Bihar ki Khabren in English, Hindi and Urdu respectively. With his hard labour and cooperation, we were able to bring about perceptible improvement in the quality and regularity of these publications and two others, one in Hindi from Ranchi called Adivasi and the Hor Sambad from Santhal Pargans. The photography section which was headed by a competent photographer, Brihaspati Sahu under the overall charge of the Press Section was energised and emphasis was shifted from the personal photographs of the Ministers to coverage of important events, plan schemes and development projects. The film section though headed by a reputed cine cameraman of Bombay, Shri Dronacharya continued limping for several months as it was under the charge of Addl, Director, Mahi Narayan Jha. However, I energised it by and by and when it shook off the lethargy, we were able to produce a beautiful coloured documentary 'The Adivasies of Bihar'! My favourite, project of producing a feature cum documentary film 'Bihar through the Ages' however, could not see the light of the day because the great 'Bihar Famine' of 1967 came soon after the project was mooted and all our efforts were directed towards fighting the drought.

The year 1967 is a landmark in the political life of

Bihar and of some other states, because for the first time after independence the solid hold of the Congress party cracked up here and there and for the first time after Independence we got in this state a non Congress government—the United Front Govt. as it came to be called—comprising Socialists, Communists, Jansangh, Jamate party which later on became a part of BLD It was a Government of various parties all in opposition to the Congress who had combined together and got a majority in the Bihar Assembly. The United Front Government of which Shri Mahamaya Prassad Sinha, an Ex-Congressman of Saran District who had defeated the erstwhile Chief Minister, Shri K.B, Sahay, was the Chief Minister and Shri Karpoori Thakur, who became the Chief Minister of Bihar after the Congress rout in the general election of 1977, was the Dy. Chief Minister, had ministers from the Socialist Party, the CPI, the Praja Socialist Party, the Jan Sangh and the Janata Party of Ramgarh, a big Zamindar in the district of Hazaribagh. In this Govt. Mr. Hasibur Rahman, a lawyer of Purnea became my Minister from out of the PSP Group.

The United Front Govt, in Bihar like the Janata Govt. in the Centre after they swept to power in 1977, was a house divided from within and the Ministers often spoke in different voices. There was a scramble for personal publicity and demands from most Ministers for an Information Officer to undertake his 'personal' publicity. Every Minister with the solitary exception of Shri Karpoori Thakur wanted his photograph to appear in the newspaper every day, if possible. Bhola Prasad Singh, Minister for Local Self Government selected a young PRD Assistant Director and wanted me to attach the young man to him to go out with him on tours. There was quite a row when I refused the request and plainly told him that if he wanted this man or any body in particular to be earmarked for him to accompany him on tours, he should first get a post created for this purpose. I also told him that since there are officers of the PRD posted in each district, and even in the sub-divisions, they could be utilised for genuine publicity work wherever the Minister might require them to do so. Then there was the Police Minister, Ramanand

Tewary. He was a semi-educated man having risen from the rank of a Police Constable. He used to be thrilled whenever a photograph of him appeared in any newspaper, and the photographic section of the PRD had to spend hours making numerous copies of the photograph for the Minister's Consumption.

The United Front Government, however, did commendable work in tackling the great famine of 1967. All the Ministers started touring intensively in the areas allotted to each by the Cabinet and the entire administration was geared towards tackling the calamity on war footing. Thousands of feeding centres were opened, tens of thousands of surface wells were dug and ground water exploration in the dry hilly zones were undertaken extensively for the first time in the state. A special committee of the Cabinet under the chairmanship of Shri Kapildeo Singh, Supply Minister from Barahaiya in Monghyr district functioned as the Monitoring Committee. The Committee met on every Tuesday, and besides the Ministers, the Chief Secretary and the Development Commissioner were invariably present. I was also required to attend all the meetings of the Committee to ensure quick publicity to the decisions taken soon ofter the meetings. The Supply Minister also briefed the press. He had all the relevant facts and figures at his finger tips. He worked hard and his knowledge of even minor details in the remote areas of the districts was remarkable.

With the famine looming large, the work of the Public Relations Department increased enormously. We issued press releases every day and some times I had even to personally brief the press on how things were taking shape in the different areas, and what efforts were being made by the Government and the non-governmental agencies to fight the drought. This was not all. Reporters from all over the world flocked to Patna to see things for themselves, and I had a hard time convincing some of them that human corpses were not lying on the streets of Patna and elsewhere, as flashed by a plucky journalist from America. For ready reference and for keeping a watch on the progress of relief operations, I had in my office room several boards giving statistics of progress of various schemes to fight the famine. The figures were updated every week and some of them even everyday. We gave publicity of the extent of the famine, and what was being done to tackle it. We brought out in record time a beautiful brochure "Bihar Fights The Drought" which was acclaimed all over the country and even attracted notice in foreign countries. A notable visitor was the Editor of a Canadian monthly journal who spent the whole day with me in the office and even made a call at my house to thank us for briefing him with so such facts and details regarding the famine. I still remember that when he came to my house we treated him with some typical Bihari food which he said he would remember long after he would fly back home.

When I look back to these eventful days I feel that whereever one might be—to whatever station of life one may be placed in—one can always do his best to help his fellowmen, and though doling out food and money to the needy may be the primary need of the hour, sustaining the sagging morale of the population by giving out correct and encouraging news has its own role to play. By projecting the famine and the massive efforts made to tackle the enormous problem, the PRD did a signal service to the state, and I take some pride in having been associated with it at that critical juncture in the life of this state.

Even though not directly concerned with this narrative, my mind inescapably turns to the most valuable contribution made by the Bihar Relief Committee of which Shri Jai Prakash Narayan was the Chairman, in organising relief operations in the countryside. No non-governmental agency during my memory has worked with such selfless zeal and devotion in the cause of the suffering humanity as the Bihar Relief Committee did under the wholetime guidance and supervision of the Lok Nayak. This, however, is all history as the Lok Nayak is no more and the Bihar Relief Committee which still exists is no longer a focus of any special attention.

With the passing away of the acute stage of the drought, the petty demands of the Ministers, their craze for personal publicity, their anxiety to favour their friends and relations again surfaced. The Information Minister, Hasibur Rahman wanted a certain gentleman to be appointed to the post of Literature officer in the PRD which had been lying vacant for some time. He spoke to me and expressed the desire that the particular gentleman should be appointed to the post. The man he wanted me to appoint was quite good but he had not applied for the job when the post had been advertised last. I told the Minister that we would advertise the post again and if this man applied for it his case would be considered along with others and I hoped that in view of his qualifications there was a fair chance of his being appointed. But the Minister was in no mood to wait and let this routine go through the mill. He issued an order on the file saying that "So and so is appointed to the post of Literature officer." I sent it, to the Secretary saying that if the Minister's orders had to be complied with at all, it has to be at the secretariat level, as the secretariat officers alone were authorised to authenticate Ministers' orders, which are government orders. This was a very inconvenient proposition for the Secretary who did not wish to be on the wrong side of the Minister. The file was sent to the Law Department who advised that my stand was correct and if appointment letter had to be issued in compliance with the Minister's order on the file, the appropriate officer to do so was the Secretary or Dy. Secretary/Under Secretary, and not the Head of the Department. But to please the Minister who was also the Law Minister, the Law Department also noted in the file that if the DPR i.e. myself, considered the Minister's Minutes as his advice, and not an order, the DPR could on his own issue the appointment letter as the DPR was the appointing authority for the post. I wrote that what the Minister had written could not by any stretch of imagination be construed as his advice, and so the question of my issuing the appointment letter did not arise. The matter was allowed to rest at that. But when I proceeded on two months leave to visit my relations in Assam, Mahi Narayan Jha, who officiated as Director in the leave vacancy, succumbed to the pressure of the Minister and the person was appointed to the post. This deal of the Ministers came in for a lot of criticism and was the subject matter of a severe indictment by the Mudholkar Commission of Enquiry which was appointed by the Congress Government after the fall of the United Front Government, to enquire into the irregularities of the Ministers of the erstwhile United Front Government.

Before passing on to my next tenure which coincided more or less with the exit of the United Front Government, I must say a few words regarding my assessment of the overall picture and performance of the United Front Government. When the United Front Government came to power, people were full of hopes. The new faces on the ministerial gaddy Sarvashri Karpoori Thakur, Indradeep Sinha, Chandra Sekhar Singh, Kapildeo Singh and Ramanand Tiwari and others presented a clean and progressive image untainted by the lure of power and pelf, and a great enthusiasm was witnessed among the people that the age of money power and casteism was over and people could look forward to a period of progress and prosperity and the end of favouritism, nepotism and corruption. But their hopes were soon belied. The United Front Ministers were free from corruption and some good work in the sphere of land reforms bettering the conditions etc of the poor were undertaken. But the ugly face of casteism which had been invisible during the period of the famine, came back to the fore in full force. Each Minister not only wanted a man of his own caste on his personal staff but also made efforts to bring officers of their own caste to man the senior positions in his department. It was indeed shocking to find a C.P.I. Minister trying to bring in his own caste men to man senior posts in his Department. Even a Minister who proposed to be a celebrated Praja Socialist leader and a trade unionist of repute did not measure up to his reputation. Another feature of their tenure was the constant bickering going on among the Ministers and their party men leading often to Chaos and confusion; and no tears were shed when the United Front Government went out of office and President's rule was imposed on Bihar.

It would not be out of place to mention here that it was during this period that I was selected for an appointment in the Government of India as a Deputy Secretary in the Ministry of Education, which I was unable to avail of due to my wife's continued illness.

7

Supply and Commerce and Board of Revenue

I was transferred from the PRD as Additional Secretary in the Supply and Commerce Department in August 1968 and served there for about a year. Shri R.S. Mandal who later became the Chief Secretary (when Sri Saroga Pd. Rai was the Chief Minister) was the Food Commissioner and Shri Rameshwar Nath was the Secretary of the Department. Shri Mandal and Sri Nath were close friends. While Sri Rameshwar Nath was an easy going man, Sri Mandal was a good officer by all accounts and his approach to problem was often progmatic and generally fair. He had only one noticeable weakness, which is these days an asset, and that was to keep an the right side of the bosses. This was the period when Bihar was passing through a spell of President's rule. Sri M.S. Rao (Retd. I.C.S.) an ex-Chief Secretary of Bihar was one of the Advisers to the Governor of Bihar, Govt. of India had sought the opinion of the State Government regarding the fixation of quota of Sugar to be released for sale through fair price shops and the percentage to be left to the mills for sale in the open market. There was a difference of opinion between me and Sri Mandal regarding the fixation of quota to be released for sale through fair price shops. While I was advocating a higher percentage of release for sale to the consumers at controlled price through the fair price shops, Mr. Mandal wanted a greater percentage of the production to be left to the factories for sale in the open market at prices fixed by the producers. The Adviser after holding a meeting at which Mr. Mandal and I were also present, upheld my stand and this was actually adopted by the Government of India as a policy for the entire country for that year. Another important achievement of the Department was to prevail upon the Government of India to link the price of petrol in our State to the Barauni Refinery for supply to consumers in the state.

My tenure in the Supply department was brief. The Secretary who probably felt jealous of me for the good work being done in the matter of distribution of essential articles like cement, coal, kerosene, sugar etc. which were under my charge and for which my work was being appreciated, prevailed upon the Food Commissioner, Shri Mandal and later Sh. S.C. Mishra that there was not enough work in the Supply department for an Additional Secretary, and so the post was kept in abeyance and I was transferred to the Board of Revenue as its Secretary.

The Board of Revenue in Bihar, as in some other states, which was at one time a very important organization had of late lost most of its importance and had gone into eclipse with emphasis now shifting to Development Departments. The post of Secretary to the Board of Revenue was often held by the junior I.A.S. officer of the rank of a Deputy Secretary and carried a special pay of Rs. 150 p.m. Since I was senior enough to be appointed as a Secretary to Govt. and had actually held an equivalent post of Addl. Secretary, the post of Secretary to the Board of Revenue was upgraded to the rank of a Secretary to Government and the special pay attached to the post was raised to Rs. 250/- p.m. for the period I was to hold that post.

The Board of Revenue was a sleepy organisation and the only work of some interest was the holding of departmental examinations twice a year for members of the All India Services and the state civil, judicial, and other services, all of whom were required to pass an examination in certain subjects connected with their duties before they could be confirmed in their jobs. The Member, Board of Revenue and the Secretary of the Board who were respectively the ex-officio chairman and secretary of the Central Examination Committee as the examining body was called, had some additional work to do in connection with the work of the Central Examination Committee. The Central Examination Committee seldom met, and the Member and secretary of the Board of Revenue had to do everything and decide on any controversial issue, in connection with holding of the examinations, including appointment of examiners and publication of results. This, incidentally, provided the much needed relaxation from the otherwise dull and monotonous work of the Board of Revenue. This assignment, by the way, was also of considerable financial benefit to me because I got fairly large sums as honorarium for the work connected with the central examination committee which came in handy in rehabilitating me financially after the considerable liability incurred by me in my daughter's marriage in 1966. It was also during this period that the State Government granted me an honorarium for the 'Settlement Report' of Singhbhum which I had prepared and submitted to Government while working as Additional Secretary in Supply Department. Incidentally, this report, had attracted some notice not only in Bihar but also outside the State, and quite a few people including the Director of Land Surveys from Punjab came to consult me on Revenue matters, besides a few Professors including one from Cuttack who were making researches in allied subjects.

8

Looking after Scheduled Castes and Tribes and Bihar Forests

I was transferred from the Board of Revenue to the Welfare Department as its Secretary in February, 1971. My transfer to the Welfare Department has its own story to tell. Shri Karpoori Thakur was the Chief Minister and Shri Ram Sevak Mandal was the Chief Secretary. The Chief Minister in consultation with the Agriculture Minister approved of my appointment as Secretary, Agriculture; but the then Welfare Secretary who had considerable influence in political circles approached the Chief Secretary, who due to political pressure prevailed upon the Chief Minister to send me to the Welfare Department. The Welfare Secretary was appointed as Secretary Agriculture. The caste to which I happen to belong had little political leverage in Bihar. R.S. Mandal generally managed things in such a way so as to keep the dominant political sections in good humour. During the time of Shri Daroga Prasad Rai, when the Chief Minister, had approved the proposal of my appointment first as Secretary, Labour and then as Secretary Home (Special), Shri R.S. Mandal under the influence of politicians in the first case and the backward lobby in the second, had the proposals shelved when the Cabinet Memorandum for these posts came up before the Council of Ministers for their approval. I am writing this not out of any regret for losing these appointments but to show on what considerations senior appointments were made in this State. The then Chief Minister Shri D.P. Rai, himself, told me how due to *volte face*, of the Chief Secretary my appointment in the Home (Special), could not get through the Cabinet.

My tenure in the Welfare Department to which the Forest Department was also tagged as a result of the amalgamation of some of the Departments in the Secretariat was one of the most satisfying periods of my service career and I enjoyed every bit of my posting here. Shri T. Muchi Rai Munda, a tribal of Khunti subdivision of Ranchi District was our Minister. He was a good man. We immediately established a close rapport between ourselves, and through his help and guidance I was able to do a lot for the tribals. I toured extensively in the tribal areas visiting sometimes places which few Secretaries to Government had done before, devising ways and means for improving the lot of the tribals, in consultation with the local officials and the tribals themselves. My visit to the Adhaura plateau in the then District of Shahabod near Rohtas in the early part of my tenure as Welfare Secretary focussed attention on the manifold problems facing the local population, mostly tribals.

Adhaura Plateau is an extension of the famous Kaimur range. It is a desolate piece of land, mostly rocky, and has little rainfall with practically very little vegetation. There was hardly any water supply arrangement and the population had to draw upon the few stagnant pools which abound in mosquitoes, and were fertile breeding grounds for malaria etc. The Bihar Relief Committee under the guidance of Jai Prakash Narayan had done *some yeoman's* service to the people. But the record of Government performance was terribly sad and dismal. Adhaura had a Block; but during those days there was no Block Development Officer and no Medical Officer. Welfare and Development work existed mainly on paper. There was a drinking water well near the Block Office; but there was very little water in it, which was hardly sufficient for the use of the few employees of the Block who were living there. A channel of the Bhagirathi did pass through the plateau very near the Block office and it was astounding that no steps had been taken to harness the water of the river for augmenting water supply in the plateau. A few small rain-fed rivulets could also be bunded which could provide water for the winter crop. But who had the time to think of all these things for that god-forsaken place? I had made a few suggestions but probably they, like many others, remained on paper.

Subsequently, in one of my visits to Santhal Parganas I toured the interior of Damin area and visited a few hillocks where the Pahariyas dwell. With great effort on my part and with the cooperation of the local Divisional Forest officer, we were able to open some Rope Making Centres from Sabai grass locally available as a bounty of nature, for giving employment to some of the Pahariyas.

The Pahariyas of Santhal Parganas are a dying race. They live on the top of hills, and with arid soil, and scantly means of irrigation were unable to make both ends meet with their primitive means of cultivation, Rajma which is very much in demand in Punjab and Delhi grows there in considerable quantities with not much effort, but it did not fetch them a remunerative price though it was sold at quite a high price in the north western part of the country. The Mahajans to whom the Pahariyas were over head and ears in debt took away their produce at throw-away prices and made a bumper profit. We had a Pahariya Welfare Officer posted in Santhal Parganas and some money used to be provided in the State budget for the welfare of the Pahariyas; but nothing worthwhile had been accomplished. There was no provision for drinking water, and health facilities were non existent; and diseases like malaria, kala zar, dysentry took a heavy toll of life every year. The incidence of T.B., V.D. and Leprosy was quite high. I felt that unless sanitation and drinking water supply was provided and effective health care units were established, the Pahariyas would become an extinct race at no distant date, like some of the tribes in the Andaman Islands. The food that most Pahariyas took provided no nourishment. I am personally a witness to the fact that scores of families lived on roots of plants, some of which are so bitter that they were kept under the edge of the roof of buildings so that rain water pouring down from the roofs would be able to wash away some of the bitterness inherent in those roots. The callous indifference shown towards their conditions of living is a bitter reminder of the fact that even in the post-Independence era, it was only the affluent and the vocal sections of the society which have received attention from the government, resulting in the rich getting richer, and the poor becoming poorer still during the last four decades. With the limited funds available with the Welfare department and which the cooperation of the local officers, we tried to do a bit; but that, I must confess, was more of a symbolic nature, and was like a drop in the ocean. It was, however, in another sphere that we tried to do something tangible for the Harijans and the Adivasis and the weaker sections of the society in rural and urban areas. Under a centrally sponsored scheme of providing nutrition to ill-fed children and pregnant and lactating mothers, hundreds of feeding centres were opened throughout the state, mainly in the Chotanagpur and Santhal Parganas areas. Under this scheme, cooked food had to be provided to the above mentioned categories of beneficiaries, once a day. During the year, that I joined the department, a paltry sum of Rs. thirty three lacs was allotted to this state by the Central Government. At a meeting of Ministers of Welfare of different states convened by the Govt. of India presided over by the Minister of Social Welfare, Shri Siddharth Shanker Ray, I represented my State Government in the absence of my Minister. I prevailed upon the Government of India to increase the annual grant substantially if anything worthwhile was to be achieved. At the instance of the Minister, the Addl. Secretary of Government of India came to see me at Patna, who told me that the Minister had been greatly impressed by my pleadings at the meeting and had appreciated the matter-of-fact stand taken by me. The grant was eventually increased from Rs. thirty three lacs to one crore and thirty five lacs. This meeting was also addressed by the Prime Minister Shrimati Indira Gandhi who, among other things drawing my attention, also spoke about the Madhubani paintings which she had seen during her visit to Bihar after which it came into lime light not only in this country but also abroad, earning incidenially some foreign exchange and increasing the earnings of the women engaged on this work.

With the amount so increased, we opened hundreds of feeding centres in the tribal areas of Chotanagpur and Santhal Parganas including the Pahariya settlements. These came in handy to render succour to them in the near famine conditions prevailing in Santhal Parganas during the greater part of the year 1972. We also opened scores of centres in Patna, Ranchi and some other towns, mainly for the benefit of the Scheduled castes and tribes and other eligible categories of the population. When this scheme involving lacs of rupees was put through, pressure came to be mounted for giving contract to the important bread makers like *Ferrazini* and others, for supply of bread to the centres for distribution among the beneficiaries. Since this arrangement was likely to lead to corruption at various levels in the administrative machinery, we insisted on giving 'khichri' (a gruel of rice and dal with some pieces of potato), a more wholesome food which not only filled the belly but was also very popular with the tribals, being a more natural food than the bakery bread. The urban areas were also supplemented with *Modern Bakeries* (Govt. of India Concern) bread which was not only of better quality but in whose case there were lesser chances for corrupt practices taking root.

Soon after I joined the Welfare Department, I was grappling with the question of indebtedness among the tribals of the then five districts of Chotanagpur and the district of Santhal Parganas.

At the instance of the State Government a survey of indebtedness among the tribals had made under the supervision of a Special Officer appointed for this job. This report was received soon after I joined the Welfare Department. The survey had been conducted on the random sampling basis embracing Blocks which had at least 25% tribal population in 152 villages embracing 9599 households of which the tribal household came to 6745.

The Survey Report disclosed certain interesting facts. Though the indebtedness for the entire population in the surveyed areas came to an average of Rs. 108 04 paise, the incidence of indebtedness was found higher among the non-tribals,—the figure being Rs. 149.34 paise per family—than among the tribals which was only Rs. 90.57 paise per family. Out of the total indebtedness of a little over Rs. 30 crores, the tribal share came approximately to Rs. 8 crores 40 lacs. It was also revealing that tribal money lenders contributed substantially towards the total quantum of indebtedness among the tribals.

I wrote a long foreword to the Report analysing the figures brought out on the various aspects of indebtedness, their extent, the sources from which loans were taken, the purposes for which they were taken, the districtwise distribution of indebtedness etc. Since the survey included both the tribal and the non-tribal households I got a few statements prepared dealing with the position of the tribals only in order to project the problems of tribals in sharp focus. I also prepared a comprehensive scheme for redemption of indebtedness among the tribals through the agency of the Bihar State Tribal Welfare Co-operative Development Corporation. I do not remember if the report was published. This report, however, helped me in formulating some of the schemes for the economic betterment of the tribals.

Another matter also needs to be mentioned. While still new in the department, I had a chance of attending a conference on tribal welfare sponsored by the Government of India at Hyderabad. At this conference, I threw light on the conditions of tribals in our State based mainly on my practical experience in Singhbhum district dwelling at length on tribal land alienation, the problem of unemployment and under-employment which is also a feature of rural communities not only in this State but also elsewhere in the country, their economic backwardness and their disinclination to take to non-traditional ways of life even in their own interest. What I said on the subject evidently struck responsive chord among those present for I was invited to be the convenor of one of the sub-committees in which the main committee divided itself, to make recommendation on problems, which the sub-committee was called upon to deliberate.

This conference, incidentally, gave me a wider perspective

of the problems of tribals which stood me in good stead in the discharge of my duties.

After the Forest Department was amalgamated with the Welfare Department at the Secretariat level, I directed my attention towards bettering the functioning of the Forest Department, and introducing measures for augmenting reveunes of the department. The Forest Department like the Works Departments, operated mainly through contractors, Forest coupes were let out to contractors who felled the trees and transported them outside the Forest areas, often avoiding payment or paying less royalty than what was warranted. Check-posts were hot-beds of corruption. Even forest produce like Kendu leaves, sal seeds etc. were let out to contractors, who collected these through the tribals paying them next to nothing, and made fabulous profits. Kendu leaves are used for encasing tobacco in the manufacture of biris and have a lucrative ready market. Though the then Chief Conservator of Forest, Shri S.P. Shahi, a good administrator and a sort of likeable man in certain ways was dead opposed to the scheme. I was, with the backing of my Minister, Shri Muchi Rai Munda and Chief Secretary, Shri P.K.J. Menon, able to introduce State trading in Kendu leaves, which not only augmented the revenues of the Forest Department but which eventually rose much further, and also ensured adequate remuneration to the Adivasi workers engaged in the collection of these leaves.

It will be worthwhile mentioning here that the Chief conservator of Forests who was not in favour of introducing State trading in Kendu leaves raised several issues against introducing the scheme of State trading with immediate effect. One of his objections was that the scheme introduced in such haste would cause loss of Revenue to the Government. Secondly, he thought that it would not be possible to introduce the scheme from Ist April as it was already February and the notifications introducing State Trading in Kendu leaves by the Government must be published in the Gazette at least one month in advance and it would de well nigh impossible to publish hundreds of pages of the notifications within the time available. He also wanted some gazetted officers and a large number of Forest rangers to be in position before the due date far proper administration. Besides, he wanted a number of jeeps and one Station Wagon for proper supervision of the work. While eventhough the Chief Secretary seemed sceptical regarding its enforcement from Ist April, I prevailed upon him to allow me to proceed with the work assuring him that all the requirements of the Chief Conservator of Forests and the legal formalities of getting the notifications published in time would be taken care of. I also assured the Chief Secretary that there would be no loss in the revenue and that there might even be a substantial increase.

With the help of the Superintendent, Government Printing Press, the notifications were issued in time, vehicles were obtained through the good offices of the DGST, officers and staff took up their position before the due date, and incidentally, as I came to know later, even during the first year there was an increase of much more than Rupees one crore in the revenue on this account.

The initial work for the Zoological Park at Patna, now known as Sanjay Gandhi Biological Park was done during this period. In the absence of funds which were still to be provided, work was started after obtaining some amount from the District Magistrate, Patna under the Hard Manual Labour Scheme. Preliminary work in the setting up of the Tiger Project in Palamau and the Bihar Forest Development Corporation was started. Hundreds of Forest Rangers who had been clamouring for being declared Gazetted officers and whose cases, though deserving on merit had not been finalised for years, were made gazetted. A post of Additional Chief Conservator of Forests with headquarters at Patna was created to ensure better supervision and control over the working of the Forest Department in Central and North Bihar. The Chief Conservator of Forest whose Headquarters were at Ranchi could not supervise effectively the work in these areas. Contracts were given to Scheduled castes and Scheduled tribes' co-operatives, for the first time.

An incident of a minor nature though of great administrative significance also needs to be mentioned. Even though my relations with my Minister, Shri Muchi Rai Munda were excellent, a minor difference arose between us on the question of allotment of a Forest Coupe. Under instructions issued by the Government, small forest coupes were to be allotted preferably to Co operatives of Scheduled Castes and Tribes. One such coupe was available for allotment and I recommended that the same should be settled with the Co-operative Society which had applied for it. But the Minister at the instance of Dy. Minister ordered to give it to a contractor. Before this could be finalised, the Cooperative Society made a representation to the Chief Minister. The Chief Minister sent a note to me to send the file to him. Since under the 'Rules of Executive Business' the Secretary of a Department was required to submit any file called for by the Chief Minister direct to him with an intimation to the Departmental Minister concerned. I submitted the file to the Chief Minister, and as I was going out on tour, I instructed the Dy. Secretary to inform the Minister, who was also away, about my having sent the file to the Chief Minister.

The Chief Minister, Shri Kedar Pande called me and the Minister for a discussion and ordered that the coupe should be settled with the Co-operative concerned as suggested by me.

The Minister felt aggrieved and sought the opinion of the Chief Secretary on the propriety of my having sent the file direct to the Chief Minister. The Chief Secretary called me and initially said that I should have routed the file through the Departmental Minister. But when I drew his attention to the relevant rule, he approved the action taken by me and sent back the file to the Minister supporting my stand.

During this period, when Shri Daroga Prasad Rai was the Chief Minister and Shri R.S. Mandal was the Chief Secretary, Shri J.N. Sahu who was the Excise Commissioner and a personal friend of the Chief Secretary, saw me one day and enquired from me, whether I would like to join as Secretary to the Chief Minister. On my asking him how he was making this proposal, he told me that this matter had been discussed between the Chief Minister and the Chief Secretary, and the Chief Minister had desired that my views on the matter should be ascertained before putting up any formal proposal in this ragard. My personal relations with the Chief Minister, had been of a special nature. The Chief Minister, who was a student in the T.N.J. College, (now called the T.N.B. College) Bhagalpur, where I had been a lecturer for four months, always treated me with great respect and used to address me as 'Sir', even before the Chief Secretary and his cabinet colleagues. Once when I called on him to felicitate him on his birthday, he bowed down his head before me in presence of the Chief Secretary and asked me to bless him instead of simply congratulating him. Considering our special relationship, I politely declined the offer and asked Sahu to explain matters to the Chief Secretary who would naturally convey it to the Chief Minister and also convey my thanks to the Chief Minister. This was the end of the matter.

The consideration with which Daroga Prasad Rai used to treat me speaks volumes regarding the character of the man who continued to have such an abiding respect for a teacher who lectured to his class for a period of three to four months only.

Incidentally, during this period I was nominated by the Government of India on the recommendation of the State Government, for a foreign assignment as I.L.O. 'Adviser on Small Enterprizes Development' in Addis Ababa. Though I was the only nominee from India and also from the South Eastern Asia Division of the I.L.O. I could not eventually get the appointment.

I would like to mention here that my personal relations with Shri R.S. Mandal were excellent. He treated me with great consideration and we had become so friendly with each other that even during the period Shri Mandal was the Chief Secretary, a very busy person indeed, he made it a point to call at our house almost every week-end and on holidays and festivals. We even discussed family matters between ourselvs.e

9

Ranchi Industrial Area Development Authority

I was appointed as the Managing Director of the Industrial Area Development Authority, Ranchi in February 1973, but I continued to hold charge also of the post of Secretary, Welfare and Forest Department, till I actually moved to Ranchi in May 1973. Though the post of Managing Director of the Ranchi Industrial Area Development Authority was created in the super time scale of the IAS, I got the supertime scale only from 1.4.1973 as my immediate senior in the IAS, Mr. K.M. Zuberi, could be promoted to the super time scale only from 1.4.1973, and the Chief Secretary, Shri P.K.J. Menon personally requested me not to press my claim for super time pay w.e.f. the date I joined as Managing Director in February 1973, as this could cause great embarrassment not only to Zuberi but also to the State Government.

The period of my posting as Managing Director, was one of the most eventful and satisfying periods of my service career. Though Bihar produced 44% of the country's minerals byweight and 35% by value having a near monopoly of coking coal, copper, uranium, mica and considerable deposits of coal, iron-ore, lime-stone, bauxite and various other minerals, and though the state is rich in forest produce having nearly the best sal forest in the east, there had been no commensurate growth in the Industrial field, inspite of there being giant industrial complexes at Jamshedpur, Ranchi, Bokaro, Barauni, Sindri, and so on. The state lagged behind in setting up of medium and small scale industries. Inspite of all tall talks of putting Bihar on the Industrial map of India by past Chief

Ministers and the Ministers Incharge of Industries, the growth in this direction had been tardy. Of whatever small units were claimed to be functioning, a substantial number were just paper units. These units whose number was not inconsiderable, surfaced from time to time to claim their share of scarce raw materials which often found their way to the black market. Towards the end of 1972, a concept of pushing in Industrial growth in selected concentrated areas, mainly around big industrial complexes was put forward resulting in the setting up of Industrial Area Development Authorities at Adityapur (Jamshedpur), Ranchi, Bokaro, and Patna. These authorities were created by an ordinance and were autonomous bodies of which the Chief Secretary, Shri P.K.J. Menon became the Chairman, and posts of Managing Directors were created in the supertime scale of the IAS to invest these bodies with some importance. When I landed at Ranchi on the 7th May 1973, the Authority did not have any office or any equipment and had literally no money to transcact any business. The Secretary of the Authority, Shri Amiya Bhushan Mukherjee, an officer of the Bihar Civil Service, in the rank of an Additional District Magistrate, was in a pathetic condition, trying to feel his way with no office to attend to and no residence to fall back upon. However, with his assistance, and the assistance of a young adivasi Engineer, Robert Lakra who had been looking after the work of Tupudana (H.E.C.) ancillary area, we started on the work of setting up our office in a small building at Bariatu Road and shortly thereafter moved into a large building owned by the Soldiers, Sailors, and Airmen board on the Main road. Here was housed the main office of the Authority with Administrative wing, Accounts Section, Engineering section and its Estate Office. The building at Tupudana erected by the Industries Department was taken over for housing the site office of the Authority catering to the needs of the industrial units located there.

At the time when the Authority started functioning at Ranchi there were a handful of factories (a dozen or so) at Tupudana and less than half a dozen at Kokar, another industrial complex, started earlier under the auspicious of the Industries Department. The areas at Tupudana and Kokar presented vast expanse of uneven barren lands with a few factories sparsely dispersed to disturb the slumberous landscape. These units though working, were limping towards a precarious existence for want of edequate orders, and running from pillar to post to secure raw materials to continue production. We tried to organize the whole thing on sound and scientific lines, called regular meetings of big industrialists and our entrepreneurs, and by the end of 1974 were able to put into actual production about 50 units at Tupudana and nearly a dozen or so at Kokar. An additional 500 acres of land was acquired continguous to our Tupudana area and 50 industrial sheds at a cost of 22 lacs of rupees were constructed at Tupudana for allotment amongst the unemployed Engineers and educated members of the Scheduled castes and Scheduled tribes. Under the Authority's supervision Tupudana grew up into a sprawlling township with good roads, proper street lighting and drainage facilities with the 50 sheds facing the main road presenting a lively spectacle. Kokar which had a few units, dotting the vast barren land assumed the posture of a new Industrial complex full of life and activity. An industrial area was also started at Getalsud where the Nalanda Ceramics had started construction. and another at Ramgarh where the construction of the mini steel plant got a boost after we took over the area. Enginnings were also made for starting an industrial area at Patratu where the Bihar Alloy Steel Ltd. owned by Birlas was fast coming up. After detailed discussion with the top Management of the Company, the Authority undertook to make water supply arrangement in the entire industrial complex at Patratu on "cost plus", basis; but this arrangement could not materialise because of inert handling of the matter at the Secretariat level. We were the first in the state to start an 'Entrepreneur Development Programme', a course of training for young potential entrepreneurs. This was financed by the Authority and was run at the Xavier Institute, Ranchi under the day to day guidance of Eather Bogart, a dedicated Belgian missionary at the Xavier Church. The Programme had a definite tilt in favour of Adivasis and Harijans and attracted considerable notice. Before I left the Authority in December 1974, one batch of trainees had come out successfully and the next batch was being selected. After the conclusion of the first course of training, certificates and medals were distributed by the Minister for Industries at a colourful function.

Another scheme, under 'Research and Development Programme' related to the opening of a number of sophisticated units to be run by graduate Engineers in the campus of the Birla Institute of Technology, Mesra (Ranchi) facing the Ranchi-Hazaribagh Main road. The Board of Governors of B.I.T , Mesra with the efforts of Shri Pandey, Dy. Director of Mesra, came to an understanding with us under which the B.I T. agreed to transfer to the Authority 50 acres of land free of cost on the condition that only highly sophisticated units would be set up there by Engineering graduates coming out of the B.I.T. and other Engineering Colleges in Bihar. The Selection of entrepreneurs for these units had to be made by a selection committee in which a representative of B.I.T. Mesra would also be there. This was a very useful scheme but it could not see the light of the day during my time due to inept handling of the matter at the Secretariat. The scheme was eventually implemented, but instead of being a part of the Authority's wing it is being managed by the B.I.T. with a tenuous Supervision and control of the Industries Deptt.

Soon after the Authority came into being, we had a series of conferences with the Top Management of HEC including General Kini, and was able to persuade the Company to extend better terms and facilities to the ancillary units and give them adequate orders. We were also able to convince the Managing Director of the N.C.D.C., Mr. R.G.Mahendru who was good enough to spell out some items which our industrial units could produce for their consumption.

One of the reasons for slow growth of Small Scale Industries is the difficulty in getting raw materials for construction and scarce raw materials for production. We soon directed our attention towards this pressing problem. We obtained our separate quota for cement and appointed our stockist from where we used to allot cement to the units for construction purposes. Similarly, in respect of steel materials we got a separate quota from which we allotted steel materials for construction and production purposes to the Units under our jurisdiction. Our efforts for getting a Steel Stock Yard of the Hindustan Steel opened at Ranchi could not materialize. In order to obviate delay in grant of loans to entrepreneurs, we worked out an arrangement with the Banks whereby units whose economic viability and technical feasibility were certified by us after detailed examination by a committee consisting of top Engineers, Economists and the Manager of the lead bank which we had constituted, were to be granted loan without the bank going through the cumbersome procedure of enquiry at their end over again.

We organized a two-day seminar on Industrial Development in October 1973 which was attended by representatives of HEC and other top industrial organizations, small scale industries and ancillary units, banking institutions, research organizations, B.I.T. and representatives of state Govt. and Govt. of India including the Reserve Bank to focus attention on various aspects of industrial growth and brought out a beautiful Souvenir containing articles on related matters which was widely acclaimed by all interested people including Shri Chander Shekhar Singh, the Minister for Industries and Shri Ranchor Prasad, Deputy Chairman of the State Planning Board, who presided over the plenary session. Thereafter, we divided ourselves into various committees for indepth consideration of different aspects connected with industrial growth.

Life as Managing Director of the Industrial Area Development Authority was full of activities and excitement. It was tentalising to see something being built up from scratch. The quick transformation from barren and unven land into sprawling townships was highly rewarding and provided the much needed inspiration for further work. The idea of setting up a Sponge iron factory, and an Electronics complex in the newly ocquired area at Tupudena for both of which a lot of preparatory work was done could not make the desired headway mainly due to the delays at the Secretariat. Such delays at the Secretariat level which resulted in the non-materialisation of the well conceived scheme for the setting up of the sophisticated units at B.I.T. Mesra, the Authority's participation in the scheme of water supply at Patratu, and sundry other matters were the unfortunate turn of events. These were the disappointments ; but in spite of the limited resources at our command which we tried to replenish by realizing the dead loans and other dues from the entrepreneurs pending since before we took over, we had the satisfaction of achieving quite a great deal during the period of just a year and a half. We started a monthly News Bulletin which contained not merely an account of the progress achieved but also an outline of the shape of things to come, an indication of the where-with-all to achieve progress. These were the rewards and both I and those who worked with me still treasure the memory of those good old days. And when after two years of my retirement from service and nearly eight years after I had left Ranchi, I visited Ranchi, a jostling crowd of owners of industries, employees of the Authority and even outsiders who had seen the working of the Authority during those days expressed their gratitude and admiration for us. The occasion also provided a sad reminder of the ways the Industries Deptt. adopted in dealing with the schemes which if started would have been of permanent use to the State.

Was all this due to the normal delay associated with the Secretariat or jealousy for the quick results achieved by the Authority in areas where the Department had not been able to do much was also a factor ? Who can say! But can one conclusively deny it ? Mr. A F. Couto was the Industrial Development Commissioner of Bihar, but Chief Secretary P.K.J. Menon, who was our Chairman was helpful to the extreme. It was he, who by personally meeting the Governor of Bihar who was the Chairman of the Soldiers, Sailors and Airmens Board, secured for us the building at the Main Road Ranchi to the exclusion of others, which became the envy of many for its location and the high standard of its fixtures and furnishings. He also allotted me the Bungalow opposite the

St. Xaviers School after overruling the decision already taken by the Government to transfer this building to the School on token payment. Mr. Menon was an officer of outstanding calibre, the best Chief Secretary I had to work with. If and when he made a decision on certain matters, he got it implemented even without Government orders for which he was invariably able to get post-facto approval from the Government. It was a pleasure working with him.

Incidentally I might also like to mention here that Mr. Menon was a fair minded person. He was well disposed towards me and it was at his suggestion that I had decided to go to Ranchi on a post which has just been created and had still to build up its status in the Government as well as among the members of the public. I may also like to mention that once when I came down to Patna from Ranchi on some official work and met him, he without any orders from the Government offered to send me to Darbhanga as the Divisional Commissioner and said that if I agreed he would send me the same day by plane to Darbhanga to take over charge. For reasons I need not go into, I declined the offer; but it must be said to his credit that he did not think it impudent on my part to decline a good offer from him.

10

Commissioner of Mines and Geology

Soon after I joined as Commissioner of Mines and Geology, I was invited to inaugurate a Seminar on "Export Potentialities of Minor Minerals" to be held at Gua in the rich mineral belt of Singhbhum district on the 21st and 22nd December, 1974. Since I had joined the Department only a few days back and was hardly aware of the problems of Mining and Geology, much less about the export potential of minor minerals, I declined the invitation. But the then Director of Mines, Shri L.D. Sinha who had been approached by the Organizers to persuade me to accept the invitation, requested me to accept the invitation as it was an All India Seminar which had been organized by the Mining, Geological and Metallurgical Institute of India, Jamshedpur Branch and had been sponsored by the Mining Engineers Association Federation of Indian Mineral Industries and the West Bengal Mineral Development and Trading Corporation Ltd. Shri Sinha also mentioned to me that originally it had been arranged that the Minister of Mines, Government of India would be inaugurating the Seminar; but the Minister had at the eleventh hour expressed his inability to do so due to certain reasons. Some of the organisers of the Seminar who had been waiting in Shri Sinha's room were very keen that I should inaugurate the Seminar. I willy-nilly accepted the invitation with a certain amount of trepidation on Shri L.D. Sinha offering to brief me, on some of the aspects concerning the subject matter of the Seminar.

I inaugurated the Seminar on the 21st December, 1974 which was attended among others by some of the luminaries and technical experts of Mining industries of Bihar, West

Bengal, Madhya Pradesh and Orissa including some eminent professors, Mine owners, representatives of the Tata Iron and Steel Company, besides our Director of Mines and some local officials of Chaibasa. Even though it might have just been a formality, I was later complimented by same of the organisers for my purposeful inaugural address.

During the period of my posting as Commissioner of Mines and Geology, between Dec. 1974 and Middle of August 1976 a few interesting things, but of far reaching importance, happened, which throw a flood of light on the decaying administrative and political culture which became a common feature throughout the country. The period also was one of massive challenge to the Government spearheaded by students in Gujarat and Bihar under the leadership of Jai Prakash Narayan. A major part of this period was also covered by the internal Emergency declared by the President of India in the wake of growing challenge to the established authority. The reign of terror let loose by the authorities also came to encompass Govt. Servants, hundreds of whom were compulsorliy retired on various grounds, ostensibly on charges of corruption and inefficiency. That most of such persons were really not corrupt or inefficient cannot be seriously vouched, but, the fact remains that quite a few were got rid of out of political vendetta.

To come back specifically to the administration of the department of Mines and Geology, a lot of improvement was effected in the working of the Department leading to the increase in the royalty revenues from a paltry sum of Rs. 9 crores 81 lacs to well over Rs. 27 crores during the course of a year. The ineffective sleepy deptt. of Geology was energised and its working and administration decentralised leading to more effective field work like Geological surveys, drilling, prospecting etc. I also had the post of Director of the Department of Geology declared as "Head of the Department" in the teeth of the Ministers opposition, as the Director of Mines was not only the Head of the Department for the mining section but for the Geology section as well.

Two incidents concerning the Mining Wing of the Department deserve special mention. During the course of nationalisation of Coal mines and Coking Coal mines a number of such mines were left out of the purview of such nationalisation as their names were not mentioned in the schedule of mines covered under the nationalisation laws. Whether this omission was an act of usual inefficency of the administrative machinery at the centre and/or at the state level or it was the work of some agency for obvious private and personal gains. may be of theoretical importance at this stage, but the fact remains that due to this lacunae, illegal mining of coal on a large scale went on unabated in the districts of Hazaribagh, Giridih and a few other places. There was a hue and cry over this both at the centre and in the State, and a series of conferences were held between the representatives of the State and Central Governments Culminating into the one held at Delhi presided over by Shri K.C. Pant, Minister for Steel and Mines, Govt, of India. Meanwhile, a committee had also been appointed by the State Government to determine the extent and causes of illegal mining in Coal of which the Minister for Mines was the Chairman and I was its Member Secretary. Before, however, the Committee concluded its enquiries and could submit its report, the Govt. of India at our instance issued an ordinance nationalising all coal mines of whatever description, and banning private mining of coal altogether. With the promulgation of this ordinance all illegal mining came to an abrupt halt.

It was, however, discovered that the South Karanpura Coal Fields in the district of Hazaribagh were indulging in large scale illegal mining and the local estimates were that they were transporting by trucks about Rs. 75,000 worth of coal daily. On further enquiry, it transpired that one Congress(I) MLA of Bihar (hereinafter referred to as Mr. X) was the moving force behind this illegal mining. The story went round that Mr. X had the tacit approval and support of some senior Congress (I) leaders whose names were frequently mentioned as his chief patrons. There were the days of the emergency and the morale of Government officials was an all time low. Those who dared to incur the displeasure of the powerful Congress bosses were likely to be presented with a notice of compulsory retirement if their performance had not been upto the mark in any direction or if their integrity could be easily assailed. My Addl. Secretary, an otherwise good and efficient officer, who took a great interest in putting down illegal mining adopted a rather low profile in this case. The Director of Mines, an officer of controversial nature, pleaded for circumspection and was for adopting a conciliatory attitude in view of the involvement of politicians. It, therefore, fell to my lot to tackle this question almost singly. The constant danger that I suspec'ed was that information was passing on to those engaged in this illegal mining and I had to be vigilant not to share my thinking in some cases even with some senior officers. Be that as it may, on receipt of reports about this illegal mining I wrote a confidential letter to the Dy. Commissioner of Hazaribagh Shri D.S. Mukhopadhyay, to stop the working of the mine after promulgating an order under Section 144 Cr. P.C. and deployment of Armed forces, and to ensure that not an ounce of coal was removed from the colliery site. This letter was sent in a sealed cover through the Under Secretary who was directed to personally deliver the letter to the Dy. Commissioner, wherever he could be contacted. On receipt of this letter the Dy. Commissioner took prompt action which put a stop to this nefarious deal. But all was not to end with this. A few days later Mr. X saw me and dangled before me the orders of the Calcutta High Court prohibiting the State Government and the Dy. Commissioner from obstructing the Management from raising coal and transporting them to the market for sale. The stay order was granted ex-parte against the Government only. I, therefore, contacted our lawyer at Calcutta and asked him to file a petition before the full Bench for hearing of the matter and vacating the stay order or file a petition for leave to appeal to the Supreme Court. On the petition being filed the Court issued an order also staying the operation of the mine till the matter was fully heard and a decision on the write petition taken on merit.

Mr. X having realized that his tricks had failed, submitted a representation to the Chief Minister of Bihar and the Prime Minister of India and repeatedly tried to invoke my sympathy also addressing me as 'uncle' in view of my association with his father who had died some years back. Prior to this, I had submitted the file to the Chief Minister through the Minister of Mines detailing the facts leading to the filing of the writ petition and the steps taken by the Department to stop the clandestine operation. Dr. Jagannath Mishra who was then the Chief Minister was subjected to grilling pairvi, from his political compatriots here as well as in Delhi; but it must be said to his credit that he fully supported the steps taken by the department and even directed that the case in the Calcutta High Court should be pursued with utmost vigour. This cast a gloom in the circles close to Mr. X. He, however, hit upon the crude device of trying to browbeat me, and influence the Chief Minister in undoing all that the Department had done. Pseudo-anonymous and anonymous calls started coming to me even threatening me with dire consequences (meaning compulsory retirement) if I did not change my attitude to Mr. X, a Brahmin and an important M.L.A. of the Congress party. Some of my Brahmin friends, particularly politicians, told me half in zest but more in earnest that I was being dubbed a casteist and that it was high time that I tried to salvage my good image. I knew that they were all partners in the sordid game of Mr. X.

Matters seemed to settle down when suddenly I received a letter addressed by PM's Assistant Secretary Mr. Dhawan addressed to the Chief Minister (as 'My dear Jagannath Ji) forwarding a copy of Mr. X's representation to the Prime Minister saying that the P.M. desired that he (the C.M.) should look into the matter personally and see that the genuine grievances of Mr. X, were redressed. The Chief Minister endorsed the letter to me without my comments. There was quite a flutter in the Department on receipt of this letter. But I simply mentioned in the file that the Chief Minister was fully acquainted with the case, having seen the file earlier and that there was nothing new in the letter of Mr. X. to merit reconsideration; and if the CM agreed a draft reply addressed to Prime Minister could be put up explaining the position for her information. While eyebrows were raised in the Department and almost half the Secretariat was alog with the rumour that Mr. X was at last going to have his way, it resounds to the credit of the Chief Minisier, Dr. Jagannath Mishra that he approved of the suggestion made by me and Mr. X's representation was consigned to the archives of the Mines Department after a reply was sent to the P.M. by the Chief Minister. Even so, the case was kept alive by high level pairvi for some time to come, which was enough to create and sustain an impression that some high ups in Delhi were at the back of this clandestine deal. In between the time the letter from the PM Secretariat was received and a reply thereto was sent by the Chief Minister, one Mr. Kaul stated by Mr. X to be a member of the Rajya Sabha and described as a person close to PM's household descended at Patna in the company of Mr.X, aad started moving in various circles to set right the wrong done to Mr. X. He had a few meetings with Shri R.P. Khanna, the then Chief Secretary and sounded some political stalwarts. He even met persons close to me to be able influence me through them during his mission to Patna. Shri Kaul tried all sources (I do not know if he met the Chief Minister also) but drew a blank. I happened to meet the gentleman on the stairs of the Secretariat near the portico where he was ceremoniously introduced to me by Mr. X; but I proceeded upwards after a polite 'How Do You Do' without giving this gentleman an opportunity to broach the subject. This incident must have been one of the reasons compelling Shri Kaul not to see me in furtherance of his mission. The Chief Secretary told me the same day when I met him that Shri Kaul had seen him more than once and had requested him to intercede with me on behalf of Mr. X. I do not know if Shri Kaul was waiting there after seeing the Chief Secretary to catch me informally and have a word with me in the matter, as some one from the office might have informed Mr. X that I was going to meet the Chief Secretary for some work. Thus ended the long drama starting with illegal mining at South Karampura Coal fields which seemed to rock the Mines Department for a couple of months. I have gone into the matter in some detail to show how political hoodlums try to browbeat officials in the name of the high and mighty, sometimes even without their knowledge, compelling the weaklings often to do things which they of their own would not do.

The other case related to the appointment of the seniormost Dy. Director of Mines as Director of Mines. Shri L.D. Sinha, the then Director of Mines was compulsorily retired in the wake of the large scale compulsory retirements which had suddenly become a feature soon after the imposition of the Emergency. These retirements were ostensibly done to tone up the administration, by weeding out the corrupt and deadwood amongst the Government servants who had completed twenty years of service. The benefit of seeking voluntary retirement was also available to Government servants who had put in at least twenty years of service. This measure if carried out conscientiously would have gone a long way in toning up the administration. But its application to individual officers was often based on subjective considerations and quite a few of these were open to question; and the very fact that quite a large number of such retirements were found to have been not in order by the Enquiry Committee composed of a High Court Judge (retired) soon after the Emergency was lifted, supports the above contention. Incidentally, L.D. Sinha was also one such officer who was reinstated as a result of the Commission's findings.

L D. Sinha was quite an efficient officer but had several charges pending against him. Be that as it may, soon after he was compulsorily retired, a clamour started for the Dy. Director's promotion as Director of Mines. The post of Director of Mines was a senior post in the pay scale of Rs. 2000 to Rs. 2500 and had the rank of a 'Head of the Department'. Within a few days of the retirement of L.D. Sinha, a proposal was formally put forward for the Dy. Director's appointment to the post of Director of Mines. There were serious charges pending against the aforesaid Dy. Director among which some were under investigation by the State Vigilance Department and some also by me. But since the Dy. Director was the seniormost Dy. Director, and as the Vigilance Department were still investigating the charges against him, I suggested that he should be appointed as an Acting Director in addition to his own duties as Dy. Director, and placed in current charge of the duties of the Director of Mines. This was, in my opinion, a satisfactory arrangement and could continue till the investigation of the charges against him was completed. This was accepted by the Government and he was notified as such. But no sooner was it done than proposals started pouring in for his regular appointment as Director. It would be relevant to understand the scenario in the Department of Mines at that point of time. Dr. Jagannath Mishra was the Chief Minister. Shri Narsingh Baitha was the Minister in charge of Mines, a person spoken of as a man of integrity, who had suddenly developed a great liking for the Dy. Director concerned and now seemed bent upon promoting the interests of the latter. The Additional Secretary in the department, who normally dealt with any case in an objective manner also started taking unusual interest in the candidature of the Dy. Director. The situation was that the Addl. Secretary would put up the file and immediately thereafter the Minister, the Addl. Secretary and the Dy. Director concerned would be found engaged in a serious conference. On receipt of the proposal from the Addl. Secretary for regular appointment of the Dy. Director as Director of Mines, I opposed the proposal on the ground that since charges were pending against him, he could not be promoted to the post of Director till the matter was disposed of in his favour, and recommended that the existing arrangement should continue. This naturally irked the Minister who had apparently taken a brief for the promotion of the concerned officer and who had been ably assisted by the Addl. Secretary in this project. The Minister, obviously with the assistance of the Addl. Secretary submitted a note to the Chief Minister disagreeing with my views on some grounds, and strongly recommeded for the regular appointment of the officer as Director of Mines. It must, however, be said to the credit of the Chief Minister Dr. Jagannath Mishra that he agreed with me rather than with his Cabinet colleague and said clearly that the gentleman's case for promotion could be considered only after a clearance was received from the

Vigilance Department. This was a great disappointment to the Minister as well as to the Addl. Secretary both of whom had reportedly been committed to the gentleman to see his case through. These, as stated earlier, were the days of the Emergency and one of the handles which the politicians used to dangle before a *recalcitrant* officer was the threat of compulsory retirement. As I was so well known among the official hierarchy and political circles as an impartial and upright officer, this could never work against me. But since in both the cases of Mr. X and the present one, the Victims of my actions were Brahmins, some lesser people of that caste tried to start a whispering campaign that I was anti-Brahmin, and several politicians of lesser calibre both MLAs and MLCs approached me personally and on the telephone asking me to revise my stand so that I was not dubbed as an anti-Brahmin casteist. These, however, had little impact on my views and the course of action that I had decided upon in the interest of sound administrative practice. Tales were carried to the Chief Minister but since he was fully familiar with my work and conduct and had some admiration for the way I had toned up the working of the Department, evidently dismissed them with the contempt that such tales deserved.

After the proposal of the Minister regarding Director's appointment fell through, vigorous efforts were started to hush up the cases against the Dy. Director pending both in the department as well as in the Vigilance Department. The Minister asked me to finalise the case pending in the Department which I did, holding that prima facie cases were made out on certain charges, while giving him the benefit of doubt in others. Nothing, however, seemed to work in the Vigilance Department where delay in holding enquiries against senior officers is a chronic feature, and where, as elsewhere in Bihar, money power also played a role in determining the outcome of any enquiry. But the charges against this officer were much too serious, and nobody in the Vigilance Department was prepared to bail him out without full investigation. An ingenious device was, therefore, adopted and a report was obtained through some junior functionaries of the Department saying that no file of the Mines Department concerning the officer concerned was pending with them. A proposal was immediately put up by the Addl. Secretary for obtaining Government orders for the gentleman's regular appointment as Director of Mines. I analysed the proposal and stated that this was not a clearance by the Vigilance Department as laid down under the rules and a formal concurence was necessary before his appointment could be finalised. But the Minister gave a differing note. And the Chief Minister who had by this time been greatly pressurised by his political friends simply signed on the note of Minister which in effect meant his agreement to the proposal of his cabinet colleague. And thus was the Dy. Director elevated to the position of Director of Mines.

In view of the goings on in the Department, I decided to leave the Mines Department. Shri R.P. Khanna was the Chief Secretary and I approached him for my transfer from the Mines to any other post. But nothing seemed to materialise. On my persistent asking after several weeks, he disclosed to me that he had spoken to the Chief Minister twice about the matter; but the Chief Minister was not agreeable to my transfer, as he said, because of the good work being done under me in the Department. We had started a Quarterly Bulletin containing useful information on 'Mineral Wealth of Bihar', which among other things had also attracted his notice for its high academic and professional value (which incidentally stopped publication after I left the Department). One day while looking into the newspapers. I learnt that in order to dispose of a large number of appeals number the Land Ceiling Act, the Government were going to strengthen the Board of Revenue by appinting a couple of Additional Members of the Board. The same day, I approached Mr. Khanna again and asked him to plead with the Chief Minister to make me an Additional Member in the Board of Revenue if he had nothing else in view as I was intensely keen to leave the Department of Mines and Geology. And thus came my appointment as Addl. Member, Board of Revenue which post I joined in the middle of August, 1976.

While working as Commissioner of Mines and Geology, I was a Director in the Indian Copper Corporation, the Pyrites, Phosphates and Chemicals Ltd., the Mica Trading Corporation of India, all Government of India Undertakings and looked after the interests of the State Government and the people of Bihar in these undertakings. At my instance the move to transfer the Headquarters of P.P.C.L. from Amjhor in Bihar to Delhi was given up. I was also the Chairman of the Bihar Mica Syndicate and the Bihar State Mineral Development Corporation, which had recently been set up with a Dy. Secretary in the Mines Department working as a part time Managing Director of the Corporation. The Bihar Mica Syndicate was a losing concern and I tried to put it on a proper footing but without much success due to its organizational and functional factors. I was, however, able to energise the Mineral Development Cooperation which started showing some results. I devoted my attention towards work on stone quarries The mining and marketing of marble, lime stone etc. and some other organisational and administrative matters, and took up with the Government of India the question of giving some small coal mines for working by the corporation. We, the Minister of Mines, myself and the MD of the Bihar Mineral Development Corporation, visited Andhra Pradesh to see the working of Mineral Development Cooperation there. At Hyderabad, we discussed the matter with the Minister for Mines, Andhra Pradesh and some officials and also visited some units. The Mines Commissioner had in the past been appointed as a Director in the B.C.C.L. and the Eastern Coal Fields also but I prevailed upon the State Government to make the Divisional Commissioners concerned Directors of these two organizations so that I could devote some more time to the work of the other companies, specially the two Bihar Units.

An interesting incident which happened during the period needs also to be mentioned. The Mines Commissioner was the highest court of appeal in respect of minor minerals. While I was hearing an appeal in one such ease of Monghyr, my Minister sent for me and asked me in presence of a

Congress (I) MLA from Monghyr to give my verdict against the appellant, who was the son of a BJP leader. I told the Minister, in presence of the MLA, that this was not a proper thing to do on his part because it was a judicial proceeding in which he should not have tried to influence the judgement. No such request was made thereafter.

11

Disposal of Appeals Under the Land Ceiling Law

The period between August 1976 and December 1978 was one of relative calm for me. The Board of Revenue, is the final court of Appeal in Revenue cases in which the Member/Addl. Member hears and disposes of appeals against orders passed by Divisional Commissioners. In my last assignment as Commissioner of Departmental Enquiries I performed a quasi-judicial function enquiring into charges against Govt. servants including members of the All India Services against whom departmental proceedings had been drawn up. However, even these assignments did provide occasional fun and, at times, I was grappling with important socio-economic problems.

The Board of Revenue which has lost much of its glories associated with it during the years of the British rule and has yielded its primacy to Development Departments, had been transformed into a sleepy organisation mainly hearing Revenue appeals. With the implementation of the Land Ceiling Act, the Board suddenly sprang to life, as thousands of appeals filed by the land holding class in the Board had to be disposed of. A number of senior officers were appointed Additional Members of the Board. The Chief Minister used to come down to the Board's office to review the progress of disposal of appeals by the Board.

The ceiling law under which lands in excess of the prescribed ceiling were acquired by the state for its distribution amongst the landless persons, had many loopholes; and in spite of a number of amendments, it gave ample scope for indefinite litigation. Those who lost in the Board of Revenue invariably went to the High Court in writs: and thanks to the loopholes in the law and predilections of the judges, a substantial percentage of the orders were set aside and the cases remanded for disposal according to law". Since I firmly believe that judicial processes should not be allowed to thwart social regislations intended to bring about social and economic justice, I always kept this angle in view while hearing appeals and disposing of the cases giving my own interpretation to matters left vague under the statute. I recall some cases arising out of applications u/s 15(3) of the Bihar Land Reforms (fixation of Ceiling Area and Acquisition of Surplus Land) Act 1961. Sec. 15(3) of the Act contained a provision for filing a claim before the collector within 30 days of the notification acqu!ring surplus land. A large number of revision petitions against orders passed on the applications under Sec. 15(3) of the Act were pending in the various courts of the Board of Revenue. By ordinance No. 219 dated 2.11.76, Section 15(3) of the Act was deleted. The point for consideration was what would happen to the appeals already filed. After examining the whole matter in all its aspects, considering the ruling given by the Supreme Court and the Privy Council in certain cases, and on consideration of the guidelines enunciated in Maxwell's interpretation of statutes, I gave a ruling in one such case that with the deletion of Sec. 15(3) of the Act by the above ordinance all pending appeals have become infructuous as no material gain had till then accrued to the petitioners; and rejected all such petitions on this score. Naturally, a number of writs were filed against my order, but it is sad to mention that the Hon'ble High Court admitted some of the writs, but did not give their ruling on my interpretation of the effect of the deletion of clause (3) of Section 15 of the Act.

Yet in another case, the famous one of Bodh Gaya Math a writ was filed against my order passed on the petition of the Math, but no final order had been passed by the High Court till the time of my retirement. Meahwhile, the Mahanth continued to enjoy the usufruct of the vast amount of land held by him inspite of the orders of the Board of Revenue, the final Court of Appeal in revenue matters. This is an instance how the effect of progressive legislations is thwarted due to the complicated and time consuming processes of law.

12

Last Assignment

The period of my next assignment as Commissioner of Departmental Enquiry is hardly worth mentioning. This is a sinecurc job given to persons who are either not liked by the powers-that-be-or who is due to retire from service, shortly. I never bothered to find out what lay at the back of the mind of the Government to give this job to me at the fag end of my service. It would be worthwhile mentioning that six months before my retirement the Govt. also gave me another job, 'Special Officer' of the Superseded Bihar State Religious Trust Board in addition to my own duties. This was a sinecure assignment, the place reeking with corruption and petty politics, and I voluntarily gave it up 22 days after my retirement from the IAS, on the 22nd January 1979 (afternon).

The Religious Trust Board which had in the past many important politicians as its Chairman had been a veritable source of income to very many of them, and one of them in particular had been accused of amassing huge amount of money during his tenure as the Chairman of the Board. The Board had, however, been superseded and the special officer looked after the Board as its sole custodian. In an enquiry entrusted to me by the Govt., to answer an assembly question, I found that the Board had lost lakhs of rupees due to wilful mishandling of the affairs of the Board by this particular Chairman.

13

A Peep into the Past

I find that I have come to the end of the narrative without mentioning anything about myself before my entry into the I.A.S. which was when I was about 38 years old. Prior to that also I was a 'Civil Servant' being in the 'Civil' employ of the Government and since this is a 'Memoir of a Civil Servant'. I must share with my dear readers, some of my reminiscences of those good old days when I worked in different capacities under the Government of Bihar and the Govt. of India.

There is also a purpose in telling you some thing of the times when Independence was just in sight and the years immediately following Independence. But let me tell you a few things about myself first.

The date 22nd December has a special significance for me for it was on this date in 1920 that I was born in a small house, in a locality called Motijheel in the town of Muzaffarpur in Bihar in the early hours of the morning. We came of a middle class family. My father Shri Ramrup Prasad, an eminent educationist of those days, highly respected in the academic world, was nevertheless, the Headmaster of a private school, the Marwari High School, and was getting a salary of about Rs. 200 per month. The family was, however, quite affluent by the then current standards, because living those days was unbelievably cheap, and the present generation of boys and girls give a derisive laugh when they are told that even upto 1939 before the second world war broke out rice used to sell for about 10 to 12 seers a rupee (the seer is just a little less than a kilo), wheat at Rs. 3.50 to Rs. 4.00 a maund (equal to 37 kgs), pure ghee at Rs. 1.25 to 1.50 a seer, mustard oil @ five to six annas, equivalent to 30-36 paise a seer (which is a little less than a litre), A fine pair of Dhoties used to cost Rs. 2.50 to Rs. 3 a pair, a good cotton shirting at 6 to 7 anna a yard, (equivalent to 35 to 40 paise for a little less than a metre), a pair of fashionable shoes at 4 to 5 rupees, gold (24 ct.) was about Rs. 22 to 25 a tola and silver at 8 to 9 annas a tola. Those were the good old days and an average family with an income of about Rs. 200 a month was considered sufficiently well off. Wages were very low and an unskilled labourer used to get about 2 to 3 annas a day, and a peon in a Government Department got a monthly salary of Rs. 8 in the mufasil and Rs. 10 in the Secretariat. Viewed in this background we were quite content with our lot particularly because most families in our locality were of similar economic status. Naturally, we grew in a free atmosphere without any inhibitions and there was a spirit of fellow feeling and comradery among all the boys of the locality. I was quite bright at studies and matriculated in 1937 in the First Division from the Marwari High School, Muzaffarpur securing the second position in the then Patna University in order of merit. Patna University was the only University in the province those days and the schools and colleges in Orissa which till 1937 was a part of the province of Bihar and Orissa were also affiliated to the Patna University. I missed the first position only by a few marks because my mathematics was rather poor and I did not do well in it at the examination. I did my intermediate in Arts from the G.B.B. College and my B.A. (Hons.) and M.A. in Economics from the Patna College in 1943. My academic record at these examinations were not of that high standard as in my matriculation but were good enough to be considered as one of the toppers in my subject in the college and the university.

Here I am tempted to recount a few incidents which excited my imagination both in my school days as well as in my college. In the beginning of the thirtees the non-cooperation movement was in full swing and the whole country was plunged in feverish political unrest. The cries of "Bharat Mata Ki Jai", "Mahatma Gandhi Ki Jai" and "Bande Matrum" rent the skies and had an electric effect. Hartals, boycott of British goods including burning of British made fabrics—cotton, woollen etc., picketing of wine shops were the order of the day and the student community was also involved in the movement directly or indirectly. The shooting down of a young man Bhagwan Das at Muzaffarpur on the 26th January 1931, and the gunning down of the seven students in front of the Assembly Gate on the 11th August, 1942 (in the memory of which the Shahid Smarak has been built) still remain fresh in my memory. I was also among the huge procession which had crowded near the Assembly Gate, and one of the seven students who fell in the Police firing was standing next to a friend of mine standing by my side.

Another incident which has left a deep imprint on my mind came in March 1940 when I was involved with the Meeting of the Congress Working Committee held at Patna. Though I had got involved with it in a small way, I feel as if I am participating in the whole show all over again. Since this involvement provided me with an opportunity to come in contact with some of the greatest personalities of the age, including Mahatma Gandhi, Pandit Jawaharlal Nehru, Dr. Rajendra Prasad, Sardar Vallabhbhai Patel, Maulana Abul Kalam Azad, Mr. C. Rajagopalachari and Sarojini Naidu, I have felt tempted to share some of my thoughts and experiences with our young friends who have been denied this privilege.

Those were the days of the Second World War. India which was still a dependency of Great Britain was declared to be at war by the Viceroy, doing so without any reference to the Central Legislature and provincial governments which were under popular rule. The Congress Working Committee objected to this action of the Government but offered cooperation in the war effort if leaders of public opinion were associated with the government in a real way and a specific promise was made with regard to the country's independence after the war.

Since negotiations with the government did not lead to any satisfactory results, the Congress governments, which were functioning in eight out of eleven provinces in India, resigned.

The annual session of the Congress was to be held at Ramgarh in March 1940 ro take stock of the situation and formulate the future course of action. As usual, a meeting of the Working Committee had been called as in Patna.

I was then a student of third year in Patna College and was a boarder of the Minto Hindu Hostel. A few days before the Working Committee was to meet, Mr. Nawal Kishore Gour, then a lecturer in B.N. College (he later became Chairman of the University Service Commission), came to see me and told me that Dr. Rajendra Prasad had suggested that two decent college boys should be invited to serve as volunteers to do odd jobs in connection with the Working Committee meeting and for running errands for the leaders.

Mr. Gour asked whether I would like to avail of the opportunity (as I was a scholarship holder and this involved a certain element of risk) and if so I could volunteer and take along a friend whom I considered useful. Since I considered this as a great privilege I jumped at the offer and presented myself at Sadaquat Ashram with a friend of mine, Bhagwat Narain Tiwary (who recently retired as district judge) the following day to seek detailed instructions regarding our duties, etc.

We were presented before Rajen Babu who greeted us affectionately and explained our duties. While my work consisted of taking Gandhiji's food from the main building of Sadaquat Ashram to his room where he would be staying, and to serve tea etc. at the meeting of the Working Committee, Tiwary was to serve tea to the leaders staying in Sadaquat Ashram in their rooms and do odd jobs for them.

Rajen Babu told his Secretary, Mathura Babu in our presence that since we were also guests, we were to take our meals along with the leaders. Since this was something unexpected, I was full of excitement at the prospect of having lunch and dinner with leaders.

Except Pandit Nehru, Maulana Azad and Sarojini Naidu who stayed elsewhere, all the other members of the Working Committee, Sardar Patel, Mr, Rajagopalachari, Dr. B.C. Roy, Dr. Pattabhi Sitaramaiya, Mr. P.C. Ghosh and a few others stayed at Sadaquat Ashram. Gandhiji also stayed in a separate cottage in the same premises.

I vividly recollect that once when the meeting was in progress and Gandhiji had just entered the meeting hall, I carried tea and snacks to the meeting. And in my curiosity to know what was being discussed, I purposely delayed depositing the tray at the place where discussions were going on. Pandit Nehru flared up and asked me to leave immediately after putting aside the tray.

But as I used to go to the place twice or thrice during the course of the day, I had some idea of the behaviour of the members, their thinking pattern etc. I once noticed Sardar Patel, the Iron Man of the Congress, whose exterior denoted extreme gravity and grim determination indulging in innocent pranks. When the members were in the thick of serious discussion, the Sardar took out some pebbles from his pocket and stealthily threw one or two at the gentleman who was speaking.

I became curious to know whether he did it once for some reason or was it his normal habit to do so in order to create a lively and tension-free atmosphere. I, therefore, tried to peep in sometimes and to my surprise I found the Sardar indulging in this innocent game whenever the discussion became serious. This seemingly childish prank throws some light on the lighter side of Sardar's character.

Pandit Nehru always maintained a serious profile and Maulana Azad frequently asked some member to explain clearly to him what was being said in English. Mahatma Gandhi, who invariably came when the sitting was about to end, spoke little but always said the final word on the subject. Rajen Babu, the host used to be coming in and going out occasionally as he was busy preparing draft resolutions. Sarojini Naidu was always full of zest and often cut jokes with Gandhiji.

The lunch hour used to be an occasion for supreme joy for us. We were invariably made to sit between two members of the Working Committee. Lunch was served on the floor in typical Indian fashion and we were regaled with anecdotes and juicy talks among the leaders in which we often found ourselves being involved.

On one occasion, I found myself sitting between Sardar Patel and Mr. Rajagopalachari. The Sardar was in a hilarious mood and started cutting jokes with his colleagues and even made us join in his light conversation. Addressing us in particular while we were eating he said : "Do you know that Rajaji does not know Hindi and mest speak in English only. You young boys should force him to speak in Hindi." Mr. Rajagopalachari quipped and asked me what was my age and where I was studying. I told him that I was a B.A. student (III year) in Patna College and was still in my teens, he jocularly told me that he would be prepared to learn Hindi if I could teach, him within the two days that he would be in Patna. Sardar had a derisive laugh and atonce told me: "No, no, do not undertake this task. Rajaji is very poor at learning any language" and all others laughed together.

On another occasion, Sardar Patel asked Dr. Roy and Mr. P.C. Ghosh : "Why is that while all of us 'drink' water. Bengalis 'eat' it as they say 'jaul khabo,' not 'jaul piwo' and before anybody could reply he himself blurted out : "You know in Bengal, water is full of worms and insects and since you have to eat the insects, the Bengalis eat water instead of drinking it like others'. And the entire assembly, including Rajen Babu who always kept a low profile, burst into laughter. Such were the child-like jokes which kept the lunch session extremely animated.

I was very keen to have an opportunity to speak to Gandhiji and tried to attract his attention several times but without any success. He was either speaking to someone or busy contemplating on something or busy with the charkha. I even tried to touch him but the moment I started contemplating on this adventure, my heart started pounding and I could not pick up enough courage to do so.

Though I carried his food to his quarters at least twice and had the tantalising experience of the Seva Dal volunteers presenting arms every time I went inside with Gandhiji's food. I seldom found him alone and could not have courage to utter a word for fear of being scolded by the leader sittnig close to him. Even then, I had the satisfaction of watching this great man at such close quarters and felt overawed by the serenity of his bearing, his calm composure and his unruffled countenance which made him appear so unreal that now I recall to my mind the tributes paid by Albert Einstein to the Mahatma. It was : "Generations to come, it may be, will scarce believe that such a one as this ever in flesh and blood walked upon this earth."

Gandhiji's food consisted of milk, fruits and some garlic juice He drank the milk and the juice but ate very little of the fruit. It was a sight to see the leaders falling on left-overs as if partaking of some prasad.

Another interesting incident flashes back to my mind. Large crowds used to collect in the morning and evening when Gandhiji came out to give darshan to the multitude assembled there. He used to be always under some sort of cordon being surrounded by prominent leaders like Pandit Nehru, Sardar Patel, Maulana Azad, Rajendra Babu and others.

One evening, a small boy sneaked into the bamboo enclosure and made an attempt to touch Gandhiji's feet evidently out of reverence. Down came Rajen Babu and administered a light slap to the boy admonishing him never to attempt to touch the Mahatma's feet again. It was amusing to see him doing such a thing. However, I later learnt that it was a precaution against hundreds of people struggling to touch the Mahatma's feet and in this process causing some injury to his person.

Pandit Nehru and Maulana Azad used to smoke a lot. While the Maulana used to smoke even in Gandhiji's presence, Nehru behaved like a child before the Mahatma. Once while both were smoking on the lawn, Gandhiji made his sudden appearance, and Nehru, like a schoolboy before his teacher, threw away the cigarette after extinguishing it between his two fingers slightly burning his fingers in this process. Such was the awe and esteem in which the Mahatma was held. How lucky was I to have been a witness to all these.

When the Quit India Movement of August 1942 engulfed the entire country, I was a student of Vth year class in the Patna College and I was one of the students whose names were struck off the rolls and was expelled from the Hostel for participating in the Movement. When after a few months, things settled down a bit, I was able to secure my admission again and completed my studies.

After completing my M.A., I became a Lecturer in Economics in the H.D. Jain College at Arrah from where I moved to my old Alma Mater, the G. B. B. College, now named Langat Singh College, and then to T. N. J. College, Bhagalpur (now named T. N. B. College) where I served for about four months, I then joined the Labour Department of the Government of Bihar as Labour Officer in November, 1944 and continued in the same department in different capacities till I joined the I.A.S. in July 1958 on my selection through the I.A.S. Special Recruitment Examination, 1956.

Whlie in the Labour Department, I was selected through the Union Public Service Commission for the post of Labour Officer, in the Government of India where I worked as a Welfare Officer/Labour Officer and Provident Fund Inspector Delhi State and eventually came back to Bihar in 1953 as an Assistant Labour Commissioner on my selection through the Bihar Public Service Commission. It was during my service as an Assistant Labour Commissioner that I was selected for a fellowship under the Colombo Plan for a course of training in Labour Administration in the United Kingdom during March-June, 1958 just before getting into the I.A S.

There is nothing much to write about my assignments in the Government of India during 1948-53. The Government of India posting was a little better financially. More importantly, it gave me a better perspective on men and matters and enabled me to take an All India view on different subjects. While in the Government of India, I was posted at Sindri where the Fertilizer Factory was under construction, and then at Calcutta, after which I was posted at Delhi as a Welfare Officer to assist the Welfare Adviser to the Government of India under the Chief Labour Commissioner, Shri L.C. Jair, I.C.S. was the Chief Labour Commissioner and Miss Radhabai was the Welfare Adviser. The Chief Labour Commissioner came to like me and though my work was to assist Miss Radha Bai, he often gave me some administrative jobs to do in the

Department which was not to her liking. However, my principal work being coordination of the work of Labour Officer/Welfare Officers posted in Central Undertaking including the work of Civilian Welfare Officers posted in Ordnance factories, under the Ministry of Defence, I toured considerably visiting central undertakings and Defence establishments to look after the work of Civilian Welfare Officers and the like, and recorded detailed notes in each case which were appreciated by the Chief Labour Commissioner very much, to the discomfiture of the welfare adviser. These postings broadened my outlook and stood me in a good stead in my future life.

In passing I might like to mention that the Chief Labour Commissioner ordered that I should inspect the work of the assistants choosing one or two tables during each inspection and find out where and why the matters were pending. In course of my inspections of the tables of some of the assistants quite a large number of cases were found pending in the welfare section. When the notes reached the Chief Labour Commissioner, he called a meeting of the officers of the different sections, and since a large number of cases were found pending with Miss Radha Bai he reprimanded her. Miss Radha Bai later showed her displeasure to me even though the inspection notes concerning the welfare section were submitted through her. This soured our relations to a considerable extent. After some time, it was strongly rumoured that she had been transferred to an equivalent post outside Delhi. Almost at this time Shri V.V. Giri became the Minister Incharge of Labour and the transfer did not materialise.

The provident fund scheme, when I was posted in the Delhi state, was headed by the Director of Industries and Labour Delhi State who was to look after this work also in addition to his duties. Dr. B.R. Seth was the Director of Industries and Labour. He was very much pro-management and often used to show annoyance at my proposal to bring certain factories under the purview of the Act though in my opinion they were clearly covered under this scheme in terms of the Law on the subject. He often wanted me to leave out some factory or the other while preparing the lists of establishments which were to be brought within the ambit of the scheme. This was highly suspicious and it appeared that he had taken a brief to exempt some of the employers whom he used to favour for no ostensible reason. When my suspicion was reinforced I had to bring this matter to the notice of the Central Provident Fund Commissioner who was also a Deputy Secretary in the Ministry of Labour. It was from here that I went back to Bihar on my appointment through the Bihar Public Service Commission as an Assistant Commissioner of Labour in which capacity I was first posted at Patna and then went to Jamshedpur.

Soon after I had joined as a Labour Officer under the Bihar Government in November 1944, I was deputed for a course of training, in Social Welfare at Calcutta University in which I did quite well, and on return was temporarily appointed to act as an Assistant Labour Commissioner during the deputation for the same training of the regular incumbent.

Life as a Govt. servant those days was quite different from what it is today. Government functioned strictly within the parameters of established rules and prescribed norms, and independent advice and honest criticisms even from the lowest officials were not taken in an adverse light. Pairvi even at the political level was still an exception. Independence was more or less in sight and the congress ministries had come to function in certain states. Soon after I joined service, I still remember the case of the Muktapur Jute Mills where the State Govt. had modified, an award of the Industrial Tribunal in a labour dispute in favour of the managament, under powers vested in them under the Defence of India Rules, which led to a serious Labour trouble. Though only a Labour Officer, I bitterly criticised the Government order and got the orders changed. In another dispute between the management of the Derbhanga Sugar Company (Sakri & Lohat Sugar Mills) and the workers under the leadership of Late Suraj Narain Singh, when the Govt. had issued orders banning the strike under the D.I.R., I got the Government orders rescinded by having a direct telephonic talk with the Minister of Labour, the Late Dr. Anugrah Narain Sinha, and was able to effect a compromise leading to the workers resuming duties as a sequel thereof. In the famous strike of the Patna Electric Supply Company, I, while posted as Assistant Labour Commissioner of Patna, was able to persuade the Labour Minister Shri Anugrah Narain Sinha not to prosecute the workers who had resumed duties in response to the call given by the Minister but for which I had been instructed by the Government during the absence of the Labour Minister on tour. This was against the express advice of the Secretary to Government, Labour Department, Shri R.S. Pande who later became a Director in the TISCO and Shri B.P. Singh the then Labour Commissioner who later on became the Labour Secretary.

As an Assistant Commissioner of Labour at Jamshedpur I used to take decisions of far reaching importance in anticipation of the approval of Government, and even though many of them went against the interest of the I.N.T.U.C. which was, and still is more or less a wing of the political party in power i.e., the congress I the Government never questioned my bonafide and invariably stood by me. I still remember the case of Tatanagar Iron Foundry whose workers, all of them numbering about 2000 went on strike under the influence of the Communist Union (unrecognised) led by Shri Kedar Das M.L.A. The workers were actually on paper, members of the I.N.T.U.C. union of which Shri M. John was the President along with most other unions of workmen employed in the various units at Jamshedpur including the Tata Workers Union. Since the strike was sponsored by the Communist Union which, as the events showed, had cent percent support, the I.N.T.U.C. Union kept aloof and the policy of the Government and the management was to tire out the workers so that the strike might fizzle out and the management could come to terms with the I.N.T.U.C. union. The Government naturally wanted to boost the sagging morale of the I.N.T.U.C. Union which had more or less become defunct in most of the units in Jamshedpur and with this end in view the Secretary to Government, Labour Department, Shri B.P. Singh and the Labour Commissioner came down to Jamshedpur and talked to the Management and Mr. John to devise ways and means to terminate the strike and effect some settlement between the Management and Mr. John's Union. But Mr. John had to show some sort of presence among the workers. He made several appeals but not one worker turned up to join work. Once the workers gheraoed me to persuade the Government to open negotiation with the Communist Union. Since I considered that the workers could not be prevailed upon to join work unless a settlement was reached with the communist union, I talked this matter over with the Labour Minister, Pandit Binodanand Jha and prevailed upon him to authorise me to give one more chance to Mr. John to get the strike called off by giving him a twenty four hour notice in writing after which I should invite the union led by Shri Kedar Das for negotiation. Having armed myself with this authority which was actually frowned up on by the Secretary and the Labour Commissioner I acted accordingly ; but Sri Kedar Das who had meanwhile gone on hunger strike, insisted on the recognition of the union before entering into any negotiation. This was beyond the brief given to me. However, later on the strike was called off when some of the representatives of the communist union were also called along with Mr. John and a settlement was effected in presence of the Commissioner of Chotanagpur and the Deputy Commissioner of Singhbhum Shri L. Dayal, IAS. Shri Dayal always took a pragmatic view of things and was absolutely fair and non-partisan in his views for which he was not so much liked by the powers that be. Incidentally, soon after I left for U.K. for training in Labour Administration under the Colombo plan and Mr. Dayal was transferred from Singhbum, there was police firing in Jamshedpur which must have struck a temporary below to the stronghold of the Communists and salvaged the position of the I.N.T.U.C. in Jamshedpur for the time being.

Incidentally, while posted as Assistant Commissioner of Labour at Jamshedpur, I conducted two surveys, one on Industrial housing and the other on industrial indebtedness both relating to the workers of Jamshedpur. Both the Surveys were conducted under my direct supervision through specially appointed staff with the technical assistance of the Statistics Authority, Bihar Shri D.C. Dey. Both these reports "Report on the Industrial Housing Survey at Jamshedpur" and 'Report on Industrial Indebtedness Survey' conducted at Jamshedpur were submitted to the Government under our joint signatures soon after I had left the Labour Department for joining the Indian Administrative Service. These were published by the State Government in 1959. The Reports were obviously well received and the Report on industrial indebtedness' was appreciatively commented upon, in one of the issues of the 'Statesman' of which I was not aware until I got a letter from the State Government, while posted as the SDO of Araria, asking me how the report got published in the press when the State Government had not released these reports. This was quite an embarassing letter as I had not spoken anything about these reports to the press and was at a loss to understand how this leak occurred. Thinking over the matter for a number of days I was remineded of the incident when while attending a conference on workers' education called by the Labour Minister, Government of India, on behalf of the State Government at which Prof. Charles Myers of U.S.A. was also present as an observer, I had allowed him, on his repeated requests to have a look at the Report on Indebtedness during the lunch interval. Some one had probably spoken to him about it and he seemed to be keen to have a look at it. It became clear to me that Prof. Myers must have spoken about it to some one in the press and that is how it might have reached the 'Statesman'. In my reply to the Government I explained the position and that was the end of the matter.

I learnt a lesson not to let anybody have even a look at any document which has to be submitted to the Government.

14

The Changing Scene

Coming back to the prevailing administrative culture, Influence of politicians and their family members had started surfacing. But the body politic of administration by and large, remained aloof from political influence. Credit for this orderly functioning of Government must go to Late Shri Krishna Sinha, Chief Minister, Anugrah Narain Sinha, Finance Minister and Shri L.P. Singh, the then Chief Secretary, who was largely Instrumental in formulating and executing government policies. Strikes in Government services were still unknown and no functionary of the Government could with impunity, act contrary to rules and take shelter behind politicians. Corruption was still confined to the traditional lowest levels in administration like the police, excise and sales tax department and the clerks in the sensitive posts in the Muffasil offices. The Secretariat and the higher echelons in the administration were singularly free from corruption which seems to have been institutionalised now. Those were the days soon after the country had attained freedom and the Ministers, most of whom had taken active part in the freedom movement were respected by the people, and the norms were such that the ministers, by and large, acted with fairness and impartiality. But with the start of the Five Year Plans and the numerous types of schemes and projects in the countryside resulting in the emergence of various types of functionaries at the village and the intermediate levels, each in some way or the other in a position to dole out some sort of monetary assistance led to the emergence of corruption at the lower levels in administration which not merely vitiated the atmosphere at the village level but also travelled, in course of time, to the upper levels in administration. And such is the contagion of this disease thyt it has travelled upwards and made a home for itself even in the Secretariat and among its presiding deities. The Community development programmes as visualised and implemented those days provided more of a fun than a real effort in nation building. The programme also took into hand far too many things simultaneously, with the result that very little progress was made in the core sectors. In this state, as in most parts of the country, agriculture which was the mainstay of the people remained neglected, with the people and officials getting entertained by the social welfare programmes dominated by the Mode Mandali and the like. If instead of frittering away our energy on various types of schemes, we had concentrated on providing water for irrigation, which would also have come handy for providing drinking water to the masses, and constructed roads, connecting the villages to the nearest market, the face of the countryside would have been changed and our economy would have had a real boost.

There were also some inherent contradictions in the very concept of planning. Planning and democracy hardly go well together. One of the most difficult things to achieve in a democratic structure is 'planned developement', which requires decentralised planning and execution. This was lacking. Planning to be effective must start at the bottom and travel upwards for coordination and finance in a phased manner. But our plans which were formulated at the level of the Union Govt. by the Planning Commission sitting at Delhi were mainly expenditure oriented. Achievements of physical targets had by implication a secondary place. This proved an actual hindrance in the way of achievement of physical targets. An organisation which spent the money allotted was hailed, no matter whether there was really any impact in the field. Enormous waste of public funds towards the close of the financial year became the order of the day.

A side effect of the emergence of planned schemes was the

proliferation of employees in most of the Departments. With the introduction of the Five Year Plans some increase in the number of employees at various levels was natural. But taking advantage to the easy money that was flowing in, superfluous posts were created in different Departments with the objective of building up big 'empires' to stress the importance of the departments concerned.

Another aspect, and a very important one at that, also needs attention. Though the Government embarked upon the planned development of the country and announced that the goal of planning and development was to usher in a socialistic pattern of society, no institutional and procedural changes were made in the administrative set up established by our colonial rulers. This, among other things, stood in the way of quick formulation of plans and their timely execution; and with the pernicious system of checks and balances cleverly devised by the British to subserve their own interests, schemes were seldon sanctioned in time, and if at all, they were sanctioned at the fag end of the financial year with the result that most of them could not be completed during the stipulated time, and the same cumbersome procedure of getting the schemes sanctioned and allotment obtained had to be gone through over again. This also led to the much talked of "March loot". Time bound schemes cannot make any head way under a system in which money lapses at the end of every financial year. Files passing through an army of clerks and assistants and a host of officials at various levels inevitably leads to delay. It is time we got rid of such self defeating administrative set up and devise at least for the planned schemes an 'officer oriented system of work with specific duties and responsibilities and clear accountability at each level in the administration so that schemes are handled efficiently and expeditiously and administrative bottlenecks are eliminated. This among other things has been responsible for the poor performance of our planning efforts in which the results have not been commensurate with the money spent during the plans, leading to the present situation under which forty years after Independence we still have nearly 40% of our population below the poverty line and the establishment of a socialistic pattern of society still remains a slogan.

I find that I have digressed somewhat from the main story I was telling. But these were also a part of my experience. I also think that before bringing my readers to the close of the memoirs of an unknown Civil Servant I must also give them a picture of the administrative norms and practices after Independence and the continuing fall in standards as the years rolled by. Bihar which in the early fifties was hailed as one of the best governed states in the country has come to such a pass that one wishes one was not ever associated with it. How has such a change come about? Are the politicians alone to blame? What has been the role of the Civil servants? This writer had in his article "Has the Civil Service failed us?" published in the 'Searchlight' of Patna on November 29, 1981 tried to throw some light on the role of the senior civil servants during those times. What has happened over the years is that the concept of independence and neutrality of the civil service has been greatly eroded. With the talk of 'Committed Civil Service' started by Srimati Indira Gandhi and the conduct of Senior Civil Servants who in their quest for good posting, quick promotion and re-employment etc. after retirement virtually gave a push to this dangerous doctrine. They failed to realise what is actually meant by a committed civil service. The essence of the matter actually is to align oneself to the "policy politics" of the political party in power, but not to be used for the furtherance of the 'party politics' of the political party in power for the time being. What seems to have happened not only in Bihar but in the country as a whole that with the constant harping on 'Committed bureaucracy' and with the excesses committed during the Emergency, this thin line of distinction between commitment to the 'policy politics' and 'party politics' has often got blurred and the Civil Servant has willy nilly been drawn to the vortex of party politics. All administration today is political as it must necessarily be responsible to public interest; but it must, however, be pointed out as stated by Prof. Appleby—a noted expert on public administration—or that commitment to policies and not the politics of the party in power is the touchstone of the efficacy of public service today". But most senior Civil Servants ignored this vital aspect and reduced themselves as 'Yes men' often executing immoral or even illegal order of their Ministers. A fear psychosis seems to have gripped them under the mistaken notion that independent neutral advice would be frowned upon and ultimately harm them; and most civil servants lost their moorings and lay prostrate looking pitifully to their political bosses for their redemption.

What are the lessons to be learnt? Must the civil servants with a view to obtaining favours of their political masters reduce themselves to be the instruments for furthering the party interests of the politicians in power? In the present set up of our polity, which visualizes the change of political masters from time to time it is the civil service which has to maintain continuity in administration. The civil servant, therefore, in a parliamentary democracy, has to be a non-partisan, independent agency rendering loyal service to Ministers, which ever party might be in power. This is the essence of the civil service as visualized in the Constitution. Integrity to the profession and commitment to the Constitution would demand that the Civil Servant should clearly and unambiguously point out the impropriety or illegality of any orders and may in exceptional cases go to the length of refusing to authenticate such orders which are palpably illegal. But before refusing to do so he must in all cases bring again to the notice of Government the impropriety of issuing such an order. The Civil Servant must always bear in mind that it is his function to authenticate Government orders which become valid only after such orders are authenticated by the Civil Servant concerned. Various scandals have surfaced and rocked the nation from time to time. Could these sordid deeds materialise if the civil servants had kept themselves aloof? Can the civil servants concerned disclaim their responsbility in such matters? Even Indira Gandhi, who for the first time talked about the 'committed civil service', had in a conference of Secretaries to Government, to remind them that it was the duty of Senior Civil servants to render unbiased independent advice to Ministers and to carry out Government orders even if a decision was taken contrary to the advice given by them. This is the essence of the matter, and it is based on the assumption that such decisions would be taken within the parameters of established rules and norms.

At the present moment, however, the closing years of the last decade, the situation has been far more alarming. Promotions and rewards no longer depend on merit but on political origins and partisan activities. What, one witnesses today is patronage to sycophancy, nepotism and favouritism with a blind eye turned to corruption. There is hardly a place for an honest, well meaning civil servant. Good postings, even appointment to sensitive posts like membership of Public Service Commission, Vice-Chancellorship of Universities are often made not on the basis of merit, but on extraneous considerations. There are cases of retired I.A.S. officers in Bihar who got several important assignments after retirement like membership of Public Service Commission, Vice-Chancellorship of a University and the like, though they had no pretentions to excellence in service or scholarship. Such instances are not confined to Bihar alone.

But shall we all be a mute witness to this Sordid drama? Why can't the Senior Civil Servants shed off their fear psychosis, unite themselves and tell our political masters that it is not the 'spoils system' under which the Civil Service has to operate in this country. The Civil Servants will then have to be assured that the aberrations of the Emergency and the post-Emergency days are things of the past, and merit alone will be the barometer for determining promotion and rewards.

15

Epilogue

Now a look at the country on a wide canvas seems necessary with a special study of the Bihar scene where I have spent nearly all my life.

In the post independence period, India has made spectacular achievements in the industrial field having ony of the largest pools of scientific and technical manpower in the world. We have achieved near self sufficiency in production of food stuffs. Our gross national product and per capita income have increased several fold. There has been manifold increase in secondary and higher education. Our womenfolk have come out in the open competing with men in all walks of life. They fill the services, man the executive and crowd the bar.

But there is a dismal side to it also. Our economic prosperity has been a close preserve of the chosen few while distributive justice has been denied to the poor. Though we claim to have become self-sufficient in the matter of foodgrains' production a vast segment of our population consisting 35 to 40% of the whole still live below the poverty line and have no means to purchase food stuffs in the absence of opportunity for gainful employment, and the poorest among them subsist on the bounties of nature—the forest produce—the fruits and roots of plants and the meat of wild animals they kill in the encounter. Emergence of black money on an extensive scale running a parallel economy of its own leading to constant price-rise encompassing even essential commodities have added to the travails of the common man leading to spread of violence and corruption. It has further been fuelled by caste conflicts caused by the recommendations of the Mandal Commission.

Growth of fissiparous tendencies among the religious minorities, ethnic groups, linguistic chauvinists pose a serious threat to the territorial integrity of the country. The demographic structure of the country mainly on our North Eastern Border has been severely damaged and has caused a lot of concern to the majority population; and a feeling of being encircled by outsiders has overtaken them. The criminalisation of politics on an uuprecedented scale, communal riots, caste wars, linguistic disputes are out to destroy the fabric of national polity.

Whom should one blame for the present state of affairs? The Congress Party has ruled the country all through the years except for the Janta interregnum for nearly two years and the one year ruled by the Janta Dal. The brief spell of Chandra. Sekhar's Government was in effect also a rule by the Congress Party by proxy. The Congress Party (Congress I included) must, therefore, share both the lawrels and the blame for all that has happened in the country.

The year 1947 is a landmark in the long history of India as it was on the midnight of 14th-15th of August of that fateful year which Nehru described as a tryst with destiny that the country achieved independence after centuries of near slavery for the vast mass of people inhabiting this ancient land from times immemorial. The independence, however, came after the vivisection of the Motherland with the creation of two independent States of India and Pakistan.

With independence came a sense of uphoria pervading all through. But the general scenario which stares us in the face is one of deep anguish and frustration. Instead of ushering in a 'Ram Rajya' of Ghandi's dreams, flowing with milk and honey, with equal rights to all, with economic betterment for the masses, with a sense of brotherhood between different sections of society, we face today a picture which is a negation of all that was expected. Dark clouds of disintegration are hovering on our North Western and North Eastern horizons. Kashmir appears to be on the point of slipping away with an overwhelming section of the population of the valley determined to get away from India and opt for Pakistan while some among them hoping to carve out an independent State of Kashmir. Murders of the Hindus, destruction of Hindu Places of worship, arson and loot have become the order of the day resulting in a large number of the Hindus fleeing the valley to find a safe abode in Jammu and Delhi—all in the same of right of self determination by holding a plebiscite agreed to by our Prime Minister Jawahar Lal Nehru on the U.N. cease fire resolution way back in 1948 in the wake of the first Indo-Pakistan war.

Punjab is in turmoil. The killing of the Hindus and the law abiding sikhs, the special target being the security forces and the officials goes on unabated. Their demand for creation of an independent State of Khalistan has gathered momentum due to lack of any coherent policy pursued by New Delhi, since the terrorist movement erputed in the seventies, and the Government of India could not evolve any coherent and concrete policy to meet the secessionst threats.

The communal situation in the country has assumed monstrous proportions and is out to destroy the very foundation of our polity. The rise of Muslim fundamentalism drawing sustenance from the movement of Pan-Islamism on the international plane has reappeared in a sinister form threatening the social and political fabric of our country emphasising on the separatist character of the Muslim community. This has led to the inevitable backlash among the Hindus resulting in frequent communal riots. Ethnic minorities in the sub-Himalayan regions, linguistic chauvinists in the non-Hindi belt, minor religious minorities all seem to have bestirred themselves preaching narrow sectional interests

On the economic plane, the situation is soulrevolting. The Directive Principles of the State Policy enshrined in our Constitution says that the State shall in particular strive to minimise the inequality in incomes and opportunities among individuals and groups. These inequalities instead of being reduced have gone on widening. The islands of staggering prosperity in the vast ocean of grinding poverty is a mute testimony to the sense of apathy of our rulers to the minimum needs of the vast segments of our population.

Secularism and National Integration have been the watchword of our polity. While secularism has slipped of the rails, national integration has been a far cry and has eluded us thanks to the double speak of our rulers. Secularism has come to mean pendering to the whims of the minorities, particularly the largest minority, and all our actions have been designed to pamper them generally at the expense of the majority community, and the ultimate disservice to the nation.

National integration is not a theoretical concept to apply in an adhoc manner for solution of problems as and when they arise. It is a living, dynamic and vibrant reality. Integration is an emotional and psychological phenomenon in a mass of people constituting diverse elements having common unconscious and involuntary reactions to various forces appearing in the society which affects the nation as a whole. National integration can be brought about only by releasing such forces on the social, cultural and political planes which might work consciously or unconsiously towards cohesion in thoughts, speech and reaction to the various stimuli released in the society. No amount of rhetoric preaching unity of the nation without concrete actions can bring about national integration. A meeting of the National Integration Council can solve some urgent political problems, but it cannot just by itself provide the stimulus for national integration. Spirited denunciation of the evils of caste, creed, religion and regionalism and exhortation to national unity will remain mere platitudes unless they are backed by concrete actions, which strengthen the forces of cohesion. Unfortunately the eloquence of our leaders regarding the need for national integration has not been matched by their deeds and the quest for national integration has eluded our grasp.

The policies pursued by our rulers since the dawn of independence right up to the present times or the lack of any coherent policy on their part has, instead of stimulating cohesive forces, been responsible for impending the process of national integration. Punjab and Kashmir are only manifestations of the disease which afflicts the country as a whole.

India is a multi-racial multi-lingual and multi-religious country. The religious, linguistic and ethnic divisions are products of History. Though the bards have sung the praises of unity of the country in the midst of diversities India had not been a political entity till the British conquest of the land, though geographically and, to a large extent, culturally it represented a composite whole.

The British, for the first time, brought the country under one umbrella and kept the fissiparous tendencies under check. But when they felt that the movement for self-government was gathering momentum, they encouraged the divisive tendencies latent in the society which also went a long way in the bifurcation of the country into two parts—India and Pakistan.

The early invaders who settled down in this country adopted the Indian way of life and were assimilated with the general mass of the inhabitants leading to a synthesis of the two cultures. The Muslim conquest of India, however, brought in its wake a people professing an altogether different religion, proselytizing in its outlook and behaviour having a distinct social and cultural moves. With large scale conversion to the Muslim fold and with the Muslim rule spanning well over eight centuries, the ruler-ruled complex sharpened the division between the two principal communities—the subjugated Hindu mass and the ruling muslim brotherhood.

Muslim communalism was expected to die a natural death with the creation of Pakistan and it looked so for some time. The Muslim psyche in India was noticeably disturbed. They seemed to suffer from some sort of guilt complex for having been instrumental for the division of the country coupled with their disappointment at being left out from the land of the pure in whose creation they had contributed so much. But the policy of appeasement followed by our ruler right from the time of Jawaharlal Nehru down to the present day (the Janta Party and the Janta Dal not excepted) rekindled the dying members of communalism and with his daughter and grandson following suit, it turned itself into a raising fire threatening the entire edifice of our nation. Nehru's action in forming a coalition Government with the Muslim league in Kerala after dismissing the communist Government forgetting his own views against communal politics so forcefully uttered in the Constituent Assembly and Srimati Indira Gandhi's courtship of the Ittehadul Musalmeen, a rank communal organisation, in her efforts to topple the duly elected Government of N.T. Rama Rao in Andhra Pradseh, which incidentally had an unglorious end, gave a shot in the arms of such communal organizations.

It is also significant to note that by a constitutional amendment, Mrs. Gandhi got the word 'secular' added in the preamble of the Constitution to prove demonstratively to her complete commitment to secularism to satisfy the minorities.

The performance of Rajiv Gandhi in this regard is least said the better. The enactment on the Muslim women (Protection of Rights on Divorce) Act has sounded the death-knell to the concept of National Integration. The act recognises a section of our countrymen as a class separate from the other elements of the great India polity. It will be relevant to point out that in the wake of the Supreme Court Judgement for grant of maintenance to Shah Banu under Section 125 of the Cr. P.C. the fundamentalist elements among the Muslims raised a hue and cry on the ground that the judgement was contrary to the Shariat law on the subject. Led among others by Mr. Sulaeman sait, President of the Indian Union Muslim league and the redoubtable Mr. Syed Shahabuddin the then General Secretary of the Janta Party, Mr. Banatawallah, M P. introduced a bill in the Parliament seeking to oust the jurisdiction of Sec. 125 Cr. P.C. in case of Muslim women. Being unnerved by the fundamentalists' hue and cry the Government introduced a bill on similar lines— The Muslim women (protection of rights on divorce) bill· seeking to keep the Muslim women out of the purview of Section 125 Cr. P.C. It is to be noted that the Govt. of India had initially decided to oppose the private members Bill, but soon fell in line advocated by the obscurantist elements. The sordid drama of the resignation of Shri Arif Mohamad Khan from the Council of Ministers and the passing of this infamous bill is too well known to be retold. And all this to please the fundamentalist in utter disregard of the fact that the provision of grant of maintenance under Sec. 125 Cr.P.C. has been in existenence for nearly a hundred years in the same form appliable to all Indian Citizens without any protect from any quarter, and that even in the Muslim State of Hyderabad such a law was in existence during the time of the Nizam. The Hyderabad law called "Khanoon Zabte Fauzdari Sarkara Ali-1313 Fazil (1903)" provided for maintenance for wives and children to whatever religion they belonged. The fact that the existing laws in prominent Muslim countries like Saudi Arbia, Iran (a citadel of Islamic Orthodoxy), Tunisia and even in Pakistan do contain provisions for grant of maintenance to divorced women was overlooked. The pleas put forward by organisations of progressive Muslims were also ignored. The explanation for such a volte face appears obvious. The Muslims constitute a solid vote Bank and the Directors of the vote Bank are the fundamentalist elements who alone have the capacity to sway the Muslim masses. The Janta Dal Government under Mr. V.P. Singh transgressed all limits and openly allied with the Shahi Imam of Jama Masjid to seek Muslim votes. The disgraceful performanace of his Government in the Ram Janam Bhumi-Babri Masjid issue on the occasion of the Kar Seva in conjunction with Mulayam Singh Yadav the, U.P. Chief Minister is recent history. What has happened during the years is that on realization that in order to cash in on the Muslim vote Bank, one must pose as rotary of secularism which as L.K. Advani of the BJP has rightly termed it as secularism. And the tornado of secularism has been blowing fast over the political spectrum.

Congress men do not seem to realise that the pampering of the Muslims and their surrender to the obscurantists among them over the years has destroyed the Congress base among the Muslims and has led to the rapid flight of Muslims from the Congress to the fundamentalist bandwagon.

The communal polarisation which poses the greatest challenge to any attempt to National Integration is, however, not the only factor standing in its way. There are some others too, and though most of them seem to be of an innocuous nature, these have none the less contributed their mite in impeding the process of national unity and integration. The language policy of the Union Government, their education policy, their economic policy or lack of any coherent policy in these matters have all, instead of releasing cohesive and integrating forces, been unintentionally aiding the forces of polarisation of groups based on religion, language, regionalism and ethnic differences.

The framers of the Constitution while retaining English for 15 years had laid down that Hindi shall be the official language of the Union. But with the creation of linguistic States and the haphazard policy of the Central Government English still continues and Hindi has been pitiably relegated to the position of the second official language of the Union. It is a pity that the one unifying force if fostered carefully would have contributed a great deal towards forging national unity foundered on the rock of political consideration.

Our education policy has played havoc on the minds of boys and girls of impressionable age. The special treatment to minority schools with freedom to impart religious instructions had a deleterious effect on the building of a cohesive mentality among the students.

The Constitution enjoined upon the State to introduce a common law for the country as a whole. This directive has been kept under deep freeze and the Muslim Women (protection of Rights on divorce) Act has sounded a death-knell to this lofty objective.

The policy of reservation in services for the backward classes on the basis of caste alone as recommended by the Mandal Commission has played havoc on our society leading to caste wars among different segments of the society. If any reservation for the backward classes is to be made, economic status rather than caste criteria alone should be the determining factor. Another aspect of the matter must also be kept in view. One time reservation may be constitutionally all right, but reservation against promotion will attract the provisions of articles 14 and 15 of the Constitution. Having entered any service even on the basis of reservation, the person becomes a member of the very service. And since all members of the service are citizens of India, one cannot be discriminated against the other on grounds of caste or tribe. Attention is also invited to article 335 of the Constitution which enjoins upon the State that in the matter of reservation the policy of the state should be consistent with the maintenance of efficiency of administration. Needless to say that if the policy of reservation is extended to promotion also, the entire edifice of administration will collapse as seniors will find themselves working under their own juniors.

A matter of profound significance which has not received adequate attention is the vast dispartiy in incomes and opportunity among the different segments of our society. One of the 'Directive Principles of the Constitution' had laid down that "the State shall in particular strive to minimise the inequality in incomes and opportunities among individuals and groups" of people inhabiting this land. These inequalities, instead of being reduced, have gone on widening and the rich have become richer and the poor poorer still. If meaningful steps had been taken from the beginning to eradicate poverty, it would have led to mass contentment and would have acted as a force for removal of barriers of caste, creed, language and other differences, acting as a catalytic agent for releasing forces of national unity and integration. Half hearted measures intended primarily to capture the imagination of the gullible could not be the solution to this problem of staggering dimensions. The much publicised poverty eradication programme and the Jawahar Rojagar Yojna and the integrated Rural Development Programme have touched only the fringe of the problem. The answer lies in making the right to work a fundamental right under the Constitution.

The sitution in the State of Jammu and Kashmir, Jammu and Kashmir needs a closer look for a proper understanding of the secessionists' demands in Kashmir. We must have a been into history and see how and wh y the situation has assumed such a dangerous dimension. Under the Indian Independence Act, 1947, after the lapse of paramountcy, the rulers of the Indian States were given option to accede either to the Dominion of India or to the Dominion of Pakistan by signing an instrument of accession. In October, 1947 when the State was invaded by the irregulars of Pakistan under the overall Pakistani Umbrella, the ruler of Kashmir, Maharaja Hari Singh signed the instrument of accession to India similar to those executed by the rulers of other princely States of India, by virtue of which India acquired full jurisdiction over the State of Jammu and Kashmir. But Nehru declared that the people of the State acting through their Consituent Assembly would finally determine the Constitution of the State and the jurisdiction of the Union of India in respect to that State and in its wake ultimately came the controversial arlicle 370. This uncalled for action might have been a political necessity at that time. But Nehru made another mistake in agreeing to a plebiscite in the ceasefire agreement with Pakistan which is incorporated in the U N. Resolution on Kashmir. This was hardly necessary and certainly uncalled for. This can be rightly traced to be the gensis of the repeated demand for plebiscite raised by certain sections of the Muslims of Kashmir and Pakistan from time to time until at last we are confronted with it at present with all its ferocity. It must be mentioned that the Constituent Assembly of Jammu and Kashmir ratified the accession to India in terms of Nehru's declaration. But this did not satisfy the hardliners among the Muslims. Within a few years of the ceasefire pro-Pakistani elements in the valley drawing inspiration from the resolution of the Security Council continued their agitation for the holding of plebiscite to finally determine whether the State should accede to India or Pakistan, and there were violent incidents indulged in by the plebiscite front with the avowed objective of secession from India. It is ironical that Nehru's protege Sheikh Abdullah got involved in the Anti-India movement as a result of which he was placed under preventive detention in 1955, and after a short release in 1964, he again reverted to his old attitude due to which he was again detained under the D.I.R. and was eventually externed from the State in 1971. But he was finally bailed out by Srimati Indira Gandhi in 1975 as a result of an agreement between India and the plebiscite front.

It would be seen that the seeds of separatist tendencies and secession were sowed right at the moment when it was decided to make a special dispensation in favour ot Kashmir which in course of time, in conjunction with other factors, led to the present secessionist movement.

Pakistan has never been reconciled to the Muslim majority State of Jammu and Kashmir acceding to India. They have already fought three wars to forcibly acquire Kashmir but without success. Additionally they have been smarting under the trauma of defeat in the war of 1971 which led to the establishment of Bangladesh, and now find an opportunity to avenge their defeat and grab Kashmir by helping the secessionists in the Kashmir Valley. They are trying to invoke the U.N. ceasefire resolution on Kashmir and are asking for a plebiscite under the U.N. resolution of 1948 and 1949. But there were certain conditions attached to the resolution. The most important condition was that Pakistani troops had to withdraw completely from all areas occupied by them and that the Government of Jammu and Kashmir was to be recognised as the only legitimate Government of Kashmir. But Pakistan never complied with these conditions. Finally, instead of waiting for Pakistan indefinitely to meet the conditions, the Constituent Assembly of Jammu and Kashmir in 1953 ratified the decision of the ruler of Kashmir to accede to India and the fact cannot be undone now. Pakistan, therefore, has no case now and this fact has to be rubbed against them. It has also to be noted that in terms of the Simla agreement the ceasefire line has ceased to exist and from 1972 there has been a line of actual control and so the U.N. has no functions to perform now.

There is yet another factor which has to be considered. The administrative failures and bungling over the years have created a sense of disenchantment against the Government of Jammu and Kashmir and has provided the necessary fillip to the movement. Corruption, favouritism and nepotism have been the hallmark of the National Conference—Congress combine rule over the years in the State. The Central leadership which had practically no roots in the valley, was interested only in having the Congress-I presence felt in Kashmir and went on changing one Chief Minister after another to continue its hold on the State. The induction of G.M. Shah's Government in place of that of Dr. Abdullah and the return of the Abdullah regime as a sequel to Rajiv-Abdullah accord were all a part of the sordid game. The economy of the State suffered considerably with unemployment galore, land reforms neglected tourism taking a back seat, cottage industries crippled and the poor and the downtrodden utterly neglected. People were left at the mercy of the rapacious politicians and DALALS reminiscent of the conditions of the peasantry in the Bourbon days in France. The nadir came in the wake of the Rajiv-Abdullah accord which brought into power the hated Congress I.N.C. Coalition Government. Rigging of elections has been the bane of Kashmir politics since the beginning. But the flagrant rigging by the N.C.—Congress (I) combine during the last general elections acted as the last straw on the camel's back and brought out the majority population there on the streets vociferously protesting against the rigging leading to the present unfortunate situation. So why blame Pakistan alone for the present impasse? Can we, in all fairness, absolve ourselves from contributing directly or indirectly to the scenario which stare us in the face?

The Punjab tangle is a case of petty politicking, missed opportunities and repeated betrayals.

Sikhism which took its birth from amongst the Hindus was not much different from Hinduism. Slowly hardening into a separate religious sect, the Sikhs came out on the eve of partition of the country with a demand for a separate homeland, basing their claim, as with muslims, on their separate religious identity. This was, however, the voice of a minority and the demand was not pressed after obtaining desired assurances from our leaders. But in course of time the demand surfaced again and took a militant turn.

The sitution in Punjab demanding an independent State of Khalistan has a chequered history for the last two decades.

While on the one hand some Congress (I) leaders started flirting with sections of Akalis for electoral gains and gave encouragement in the beginning, the Central Government shut its eyes and ears to the Anandpur Saheb resolution which had sinister implications. The Government went on dithering and woke up suddenly when the monster of Bhinderwale in whose rise to emirence the Central Government contributed liberally turned the Golden Temple into a den of criminals and set up as it were, an independent state in the premises of the Golden Temple. It was then realised that the situation could not be allowed to deteriorate further and the unfortunate 'Blue Star Operation' was resorted to by the Army resulting in the killings of hundreds of men of both sides including the dreaded Bhinderwale with his core supporters. The entry of the army in the precincts of the Golden Temple was a great affront to the Sikhs and the fence sitters among them crossed the line to join with the militants. Academicians, public men and intellectuals had long been pleading with the Government to concede the genuine demands of the Akalis regarding transfer of Chandigarh to Punjab, sharing the river waters between the Punjab and other States, territorial adjustments between Haryana and Punjab, and greater autonomy to the States, but the Government turned a blind eye to these pleadings and continued a policy of drift to exploit the Punjab situation for their electoral gains. The result was that, Sant Longowals' group started thinning out and joining the band wagon of Bhinderwale strengthening the cries for creation of an independent State of Khalistan. If timely action had been taken without an eye for carving out a Congress (I) niche in Punjab the unfortunate Blue Star operation would not have been necessary. However, Indira Gandhi, though belatedly, gave an award for transfer of Chandigarh to Punjab but the award was not implemented in spite of the much publicised Rajiv-Longowal accord since consigned to history. The unfortunate assassination of Srimati Indira Gandhi by her own sikh guards, which led to large scale riots in Delhi and several parts of the country resulting in the killings of hundreds of Sikhs further complicated the matter because no worthwhile action was taken against the organisers of the riots and Punjab remained and still remains a festering sore on the country. It is worthwhile noting that when the Rajiv-Longowal accord was signed, the Akalis led by Sant Longewal came to power. And though the accord was endorsed by Parliament without a single voice of dissent, the accord was not honoured again due to the political compulsions mainly under pressure of Bhajan Lal, the Congress I Chief Minister of Harayana. It it also relevant to be reminded that while the President of India showered praises on the Barnalas' Government on the eve of the Budget Session of the Parliament, the Central Government dismissed the Barnala Government soon after the Budget Session was over. Akalis were and are the favourites of the people of Punjab. The fact that the Congress I dismissed all the Akali Ministries so far-in 1967, 1969, 1979* and in 1987, always in the interest of the ruling party, has culminated in the disastrous situation which we witness today.

Coming to Assam and North Eastern India, the continued infiltration of Muslims from across Bangladesh (formerly East Pakistan) without any effective action on the part of the Central Government has had a far reaching effect on the demographic structure of Assam and the whole North Eastern region as far as Kishanganj and Araria (formerly the two subdivisions of the district of Purnea). The large scale disturbances in Assam led by the Gana Sangram Parishad and other groups and the famous Assam Accord signed by Rajiv Gandhi, could not solve the Assam tangle as no effective steps were taken by the Union Government to check the continued influx of Muslims from across the border. The result is for all to see. According to the census report of 1971 (there had been no census in Assam in 1981) the population of Assam was approximately 1.46 crores of which the Hindus contributed 72.51%, the Muslims 24.56% and the Christians 2.61% while the Sikhs and the Buddhists etc. accounted for the rest. The percentage of the Hindus to the total population rose from 72.01 in 1951 to 72.51% in 1971, the Muslims population during the same period rose from 24.62% (in 1951) to 25.30% in 1961 after which it had a slight fall to 24-56%. The allegation is that most infiltrators did not present themselves for the census operations because their population did constitute 25.30% in 1961, and there is no reason why a shortfall should have occured in 1971. During the period 1911-1917, the Christian population rose from 0.59% in 1911 to 2.61% in 1971. While the rise in the population of the Muslims can be attributed to their continued infiltration the rise in the population of the Christians had been mainly due to conversion resorted to on a large scale by the Christian Missionaries. The rise in the Christian population was mainly due to the right to propagate ones' own religion enshrined in our Constitution as a fundamental right which has come in handy to the proselytizers. In Nagaland, Meghalaya, Manipur and Tripura, the growth in the Christian population during the decade 1961-71 has been phenomenal as would be evident from the following figures :—

Name	Percentage growth of Christians.	Percentage Growth of General pupulation
Nagaland	76.29	39.88
Meghalaya	75.43	31.55
Manipur	83.66	37.33
Tripura	56.52	36.28

In 1951-71, the growth in the Christian population in Nagaland was 251.6% and in Tripura 298.6%.

It will be worthwhile mentioning that the right to propagate one's own religion has not been recognised in any country of the world; but we Indians live in a make-belief of our own and pride ourselves being a believer in secularism which has so badly been perverted that even foreign Missionaries were allowed free access to propagate their religions with such results. It was realised even by the ardent votaries of the so-called secularism that the repeated insurrection in Nagaland in particular and in other parts of North Eastern India in general was due to the instigation of foreign missionaries operating in this part of the country with impunity. In a book by K.M. Pannikar published in 1953, he says that missionary activities in Asia between 1498 to 1945 were connected with Western Political supremacy in Asia and synchronised with this development. The position in this country has worsened after Independence as foreign missionaries have been allowed access even to those areas in which they were prevented from entering during the British days.

The insurgency in Kashmir, the militant terrorism in Punjab and the trouble spots in North Eastern India, the all pervading violence, the recurring communal riots, the caste conflicts and the language disputes are all the symptoms of the same disease—the absence of National Integration and mistaken interpretation of Secularism.

Secularism as we understand today is a product of the west. It came in the wake of revolt against Christiandom whose writ ran supreme in all matter—civil and clerical. It was not a historical necessity in our country as India has throughout been a secular State. It has largely been due to the teachings of our ancient scriptures—*Sarvdharma Sama bhave*! We adopted it as a State policy after we became a Republic and demonstrably wanted to impress on our religious minorities in an overwhelmingly Hindu dominated democracy that we mean to stand by them to safeguard their interests.

Secularism means that the state has no religion of its own and every religion will have equal protection of law. But instead of doing so, we have been pandering to the whims of the minorities, particularly the dominant minority (the Muslims). The disease of minoritism has afflicted not only the minorities but also our rulers and the demands of the minorities particulary the dominant minority has been incresing day by day. If a book is published anywhere in the world like the Satanic Verses there is a strident demand for banning this book in India and communal riots take place. India was the first country in the world to ban this book. If a film has some scenes depicting some Hindu ethos the demand comes for removing these scenes even though the subject matter of the film might rate to a period centuries before the birth of Islam. History books are sought to be rewritten and are done so by pseudo-intellectuals to omit what did take place on a certain occasion and/or to hide something which did not happen at all. In the Ram Janambhumi—Babri Masjid issue, though it has been proved by historical and archaeological evidence that a Ram Temple did exist at Ayodhya on which the Babri Masjid stands today some historians of a particular school of thought probably at the instance of the powers that be have raised irrelevant issues regarding the authenticity of the claim on the ground that Rama was not a historical figure and it cannot be proved that Ayodhya was the birth place of Ram. Such arguments will put even an uneducated person to shame. Our rulers feel embarrassment in attending an opening ceremony where conchshells are blown or a coconut is broken, or a lamp is lighted for fear of offending the minorities conveniently forgetting that secularism does not mean stripping ourselves of our cultural traditions while dealing with the affairs of the State. Our Muslim brethren must also bear with the Hindu ethos and respect their beliefs and practices.

The remedy lies in the State taking a stand of absolute impartiality in all religious matters concerning the different religious communities inhabiting this great land. What is right and proper for the country as a whole must be done without fear or favour towards one or the other, and then only will we be able to pull out the country from the present impasse.

The Bihar scene is particularly distressing. In a broader sense, Bihar is the mirror of India in most ways but the picture that emerges here is far more magnified.

Bihar which has been the cradle of civilization in the past has been amply endowed by nature in all possible ways. North Bihar has one of the most naturally fertile lands in the country. Chotanagpur plateau is the richest mineral belt in the country. Over 40% of the total mineral wealth lies in Bihar. It has all the uranium deposit of the country, contributing nearly the whole of the prime coking coal and is a predominant producer of a Pyrites, Kynite and superior quality mica. It has an abundance of other minerals like Iron Ore, bauxite, granite, appetite, limestone etc. It is rich in forest wealth and the Saranda Sal forest is probably the best in the East. But in spite of all these bounties of nature it is one of the least industrialised States in the country, and except in certain areas in the Gangetic Plains, its agricultural production also stands at the bottom of the ladder.

Though Bihar has 10% of the total population of the country, it accounts for only 6.8% of the total food-grains production and more than 5% share in the aggregate manufacturing income of the major States. According to available data, the percentage of people employed in manufacturing industries is only 4.58% against Maharastra's 16.5% and West Bengal's 10.69%. The number of registered unemployed has gone up from 21 lacs in 1980 to 26.50 lacs recently. This does not give a true picture of the unemployment situation in the State as there is a vast army of unemployed and under employed persons which would indeed be a staggering figure.

The study conducted on Bihar published under the title "Bihar—Problems of Development" by Ajit Mazoomdar (an Ex-IAS Officer of Bihar Cadre) a detailed analysis of different sectors of economy has been given which throws a flood of light on the poor State of economy in the State.

The per capita state domestic product at 1984-85 prices was Rs. 476 as against the all India average of Rs. 775 which is the lowest compared to the other States. The percentage of growth of output during 1951-81 has been 3.14 against the All India averge of 3.31. From detailed analysis, it will be found that Bihars' economy expanded as a very satisfactory rate in the fifties; but this was followed by a period when growth rate was by far the lowest among the States. The low-productivity in the State was because of failure in agriculture. The average yield on irrigated lands is a little over 14 quintals per hectare for all crops against the national average of 22 quintals. The per capita income of Bihar is the lowest in the country which itself has one of the lowest per capita income in the world. According to the Economic Times of Calcutta dated 26.2.88 the per capita income of Bihar at 1970-71 prices was Rs. 486 in 1985-86 against the all India average of Rs. 798. The percentage of population below the poverty line in 1983-

84 was about 50% against the All India average of 37%. It is noteworthy that in certain pockets of North Bihar and the tribal belt of South Bihar the percentage of people living below the poverty line was estimated to be as high as even 90%. The per capita plan outlay in Bihar has been one of the lowest as compared to other States. The rates of public investments indicate that in the development race, the maxim—"to whom that hath more shall be given" has been the guiding principle.

The political bosses who ruled the State over the years and the civil servants concerned cannot escape the responsibility for the steep decline and the present plight of the State. Bihar which in the early fifties was adjudged as one of the best administered State in the country has been degraded to the bottom of the ladder. It would appear that the calibre of the civil servants and the political masters had a nose dive during this period.

The decline in agricultural production has primarily to be ascribed to the tardy implementation of the land reform measures. Though Bihar was one of the first State in the country to enact the laws for the abolition of Zamindaries, the Bihar Land Reforms Act 1950 and the Bihar Land Reforms (fixation of ceiling area and acquisition of surplus land) Act 1961, the implementation of the ceiling laws has been tardy and not in keeping with the spirit of enactment in many cases, Ex-Landlords have appropriated hundred of acres of land by manipulation and fraud making benami transfers of lands before the date of the enforcement of the Act leading to countless litigations. When I was an Additional Member of the Board of Revenue, Bihar—way back in the late seventies I came across cases involving malafide transfer and wilful manipulation on the part of the ex-Landlords and big cultivators A meaningful implementation of the Acts at all levels will go a long way in making hundreds of thousand of acres of surplus land available to the landless people. Effective control and vigilance has also to be maintained in the distribution of land so that the exercise may be fruitful. These are social legislations and the courts have also to look at the cases keeping the objective of the laws in view.

Bihar is even now a feudal State and hunger for land pezales the entire social order. A meaningful redistribution of land is called for after abolition of subletting by big land holders like the Bataidari system. Meanwhile, the implementation of the Minimum Wages Act in Agriculture must also be enforced. Most of the violence on the rural areas in some districts of South Bihar and also in parts of North Bihar which have resulted in hundreds of killings of Harijans and backward classes by the land owners and vice versa mainly due to the non-implementation of the minimum wages Act in agriculture. Ex-Landlords and big cultivators who in the past have been used for getting work done on mere pittance rufuse to pay minimum wage leading to unrest among the landless workers. The big landlords who control the levers of power in the Government ascribe such rising to the growth of Naxalite movement and a region of terror is let loose on the poor landless labourers which also leads to retaliatory action on their part.

Bihar had the advantage of having big industrial undertaking established by the Central Government during the 1st and 2nd Plan periods. But little initiative has been taken by the State Government to set up small scale industries in this State. When Shri K.B. Sahay became the Chief Minister of Bihar in the early sixties, he boastfully declared that he would place Bihar on the industrial map of India and that slogan was adopted and repeads repeated nauseam by many successive Chief Ministers; but nothing tangible was done towards this until 1972-73 when Industrial Area Development Authorities were set up in Jamshedpur, Ranchi, Bokaro, Patna and later on in other parts in North Bihar. A few hundred real small scale units were set up mostly as ancillary industries mainly to cater to the needs of big industrial units like H.E.C. Ranchi, TELCO Jamshedpur, Bokaro Steel Company, Barauni Oil Refineries and the like.

In the power sector we have been dismal failure. This deficiency coupled with the lack of other infrastructures has been responsible for not many new industries coming up in Bihar. Due to lack of concrete action on behalf of the State

Government some big industrial units shifted their head-quarters outside Bihar which among others led to big losses of revenue on sales tax, diminution of employment opportunities to our people and flight of capital from this State. We have had a number of Railway Ministers from this State since the beginning but the total addition to railway mileage has been negligible compared to some other States. We have been hearing for the last 30-40 years regarding providing a rail-link to Hazaribagh which is now a Divisional Head-quarters, but nothing has happened.

Petty politics, casteism and corruption have been the bane of Bihar politics and administration which have sunk Bihar in a mive of corruption, ineptitude, nepotism, criminalization of politics. Booth capturing and rigging of elections accompained by violence have become the order of the day. Corruption and violence have very nearly been institutionalised. Land armies of land owners as well as armies of Naxalites and MCC are there for all to see.

These, however, are not a feature of Bihar alone. Corruption is a phenomenon common to all the States and so has become violence which pervades the entire polity. But all seem magnified in Bihar. I have already referred to the rise in corruption at lower levels of administration in the wake of Five Year Plans. Corruption is a phenomenon associated with developing countries and it manifests itself more and more as Government assumes greater and greater control over the life and work of the community. It thrives in an un-developed society which has great diverquence of incomes and opportunities. It has, therefore, manifested itself in a big way in this country. Corruption has invaded politics, it has seeped into the higher strata of administrative ladder and its waves are now touching the shores of the judiciary. The defence establishment has also not escaped its clutches orbit.

Elections have provided the greatest motive force to the rise of corruption. The nexus between businessmen and politicians, the proliferation of black money and its unroads into politics have all contributed to the cancer of corruption spreading its tentacles to encompass the political and economic life of the country. The situation has come to such a pass that even a Prime Minister of the country has been openly accused of earning money in an important defence deal.

Beharees seems to have lost their moorings and work seems to have died an ignominious death in Bihar. It is surprising that while civil servants who are sent to the Government of India, rise to great heights in their profession while they simply plod on while in Bihar. Take the case of our agricultural labourers. Productivity is quite low in Bihar but these are the persons who are responsible for the flourishing agriculture in the Punjab. So also is the case with students who rot here as the schools and colleges do not work except in name and the college and school teachers earn thousands of ruppees per month by private tuition for which they run regular coaching classes in their homes. But no effort seems to have been made to stop this clandestine trade.

Most doctors do not work in the hospitals. They go there for an hour or two and spend the rest of the time in private practice with impunity. The Government have over the years stopped private practice of the doctors working in the medical colleges more than once but have ultimately resiled from the position due to the strong lobby of the medical profession. The future looks gloomy and unless work culture is revived, land reforms measures stickly enforced and private armies operating in rural areas ruthlessly curbed, nothing much can happen for the better.

The economic position of the poor sections of society looks absolutely dismal. The much publicised Jawahar Rojgar Yojna, the Integrated Rural Development Programme and the like do not provide the answer. These work as doles and breed corruption. The answer lies in making the 'Right to work' a fundamental right which will eliminate corruption, provide a sense of dignity and pride to the poor. The growth in our industrial and agricultural sectors will have no meaning unless there is sufficient purchasing power in the countryside maintaining the cycle of production, distribution and consumption, so essential even in a capitalist frame work. Such a measure will also lead to lessening of tension between castes and classes, and to reduction in religious and communal disputes which plague the country and usher in an era of peace and prosperity. We must always remember that poverty anywhere is a danger to prosperity every where.

Things have been going astray in different spheres of our national life and we have come to such a pass that it seems difficult to salvage the position. But all is not lost yet. Corruption leading to criminalisation of politics and emergence of violence on an unprecedented scale has to be taken care of. The laws of the country and the established norms of administration must be observed by one and all and any deviation from the established rules out of fear or favour should be dealt with severely. The guilty must be tried in an open court and deterrent punishment must be meted out to the offenders to provide an example for all to see. We have in such cases to start from the top and not confine ourselves to small fries or find a scope goat. People acting by proxy have to be dealt with along with those whose proxy they are playing.

A ceiling on election expenses with a statutory obligation to disclose the sources of expenses are some of the measures which should be adopted to eliminate or atleast reduce corruption and criminalisation of politics If the cancer of corruption is successfully removed most of the ills afflicting our body politic will die a natural death. But it will not be possible to achieve this end unless there is a political will at the top 'Double Speak' and 'double deal' must top and events be allowed to take their normal course in the spirit of our constribution and our laws keeping in view the good of the community. With given determination and firmness, one can hope that things will improve and most of the vaxed questions playing the country will be solved at no distant date.

Solution of economic problem of the people cannot wait any longer. Distributive justice is the call of the hour. Once every individual is assured of his minimum needs by making right to work a fundamental right under the Constitution the evil of communalism, casteism, linguistic and ethnic problems will disappear. This will generate a feeling of contentment and dignity and release forces which will usher in an era of peace and prosperity.

Index